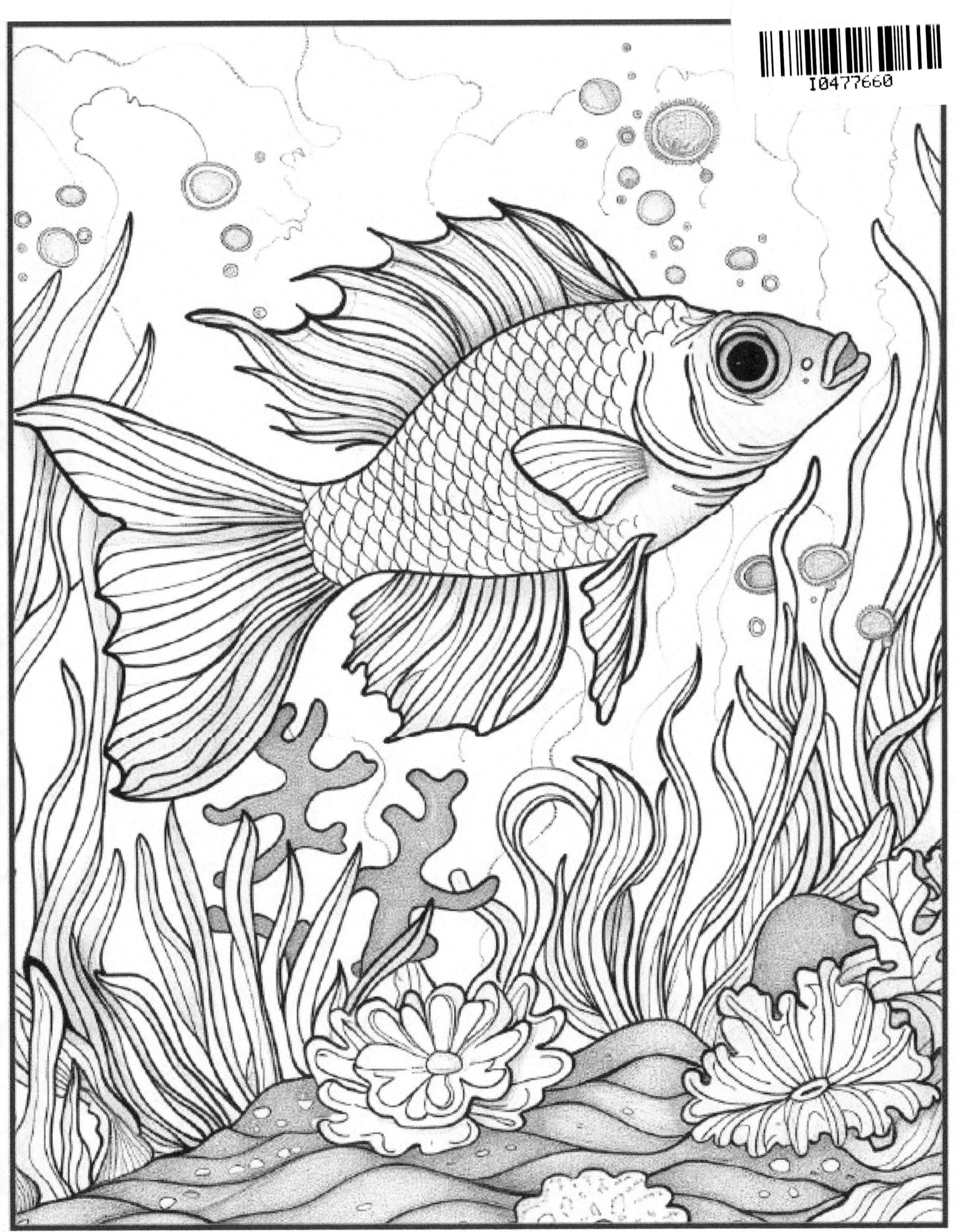

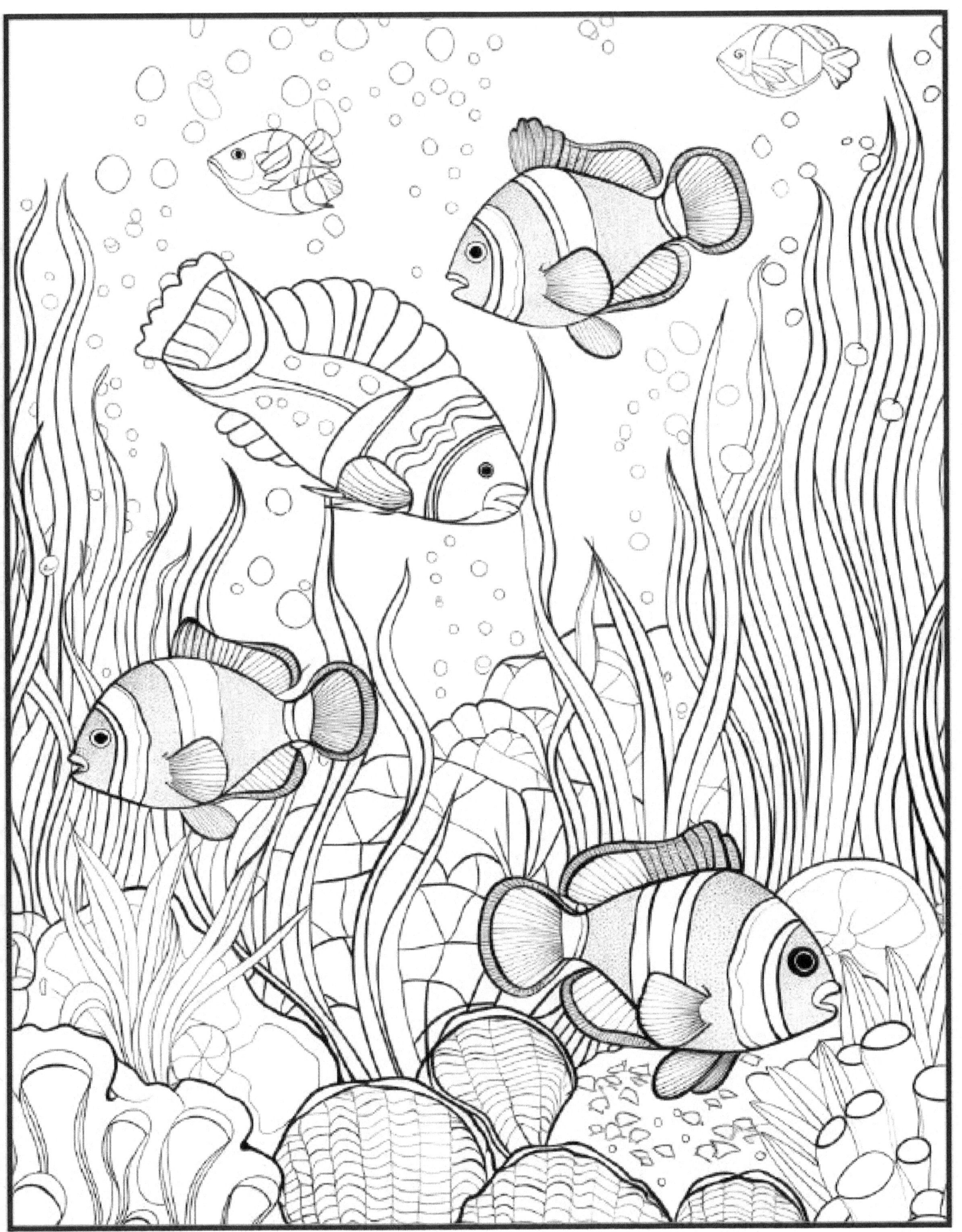

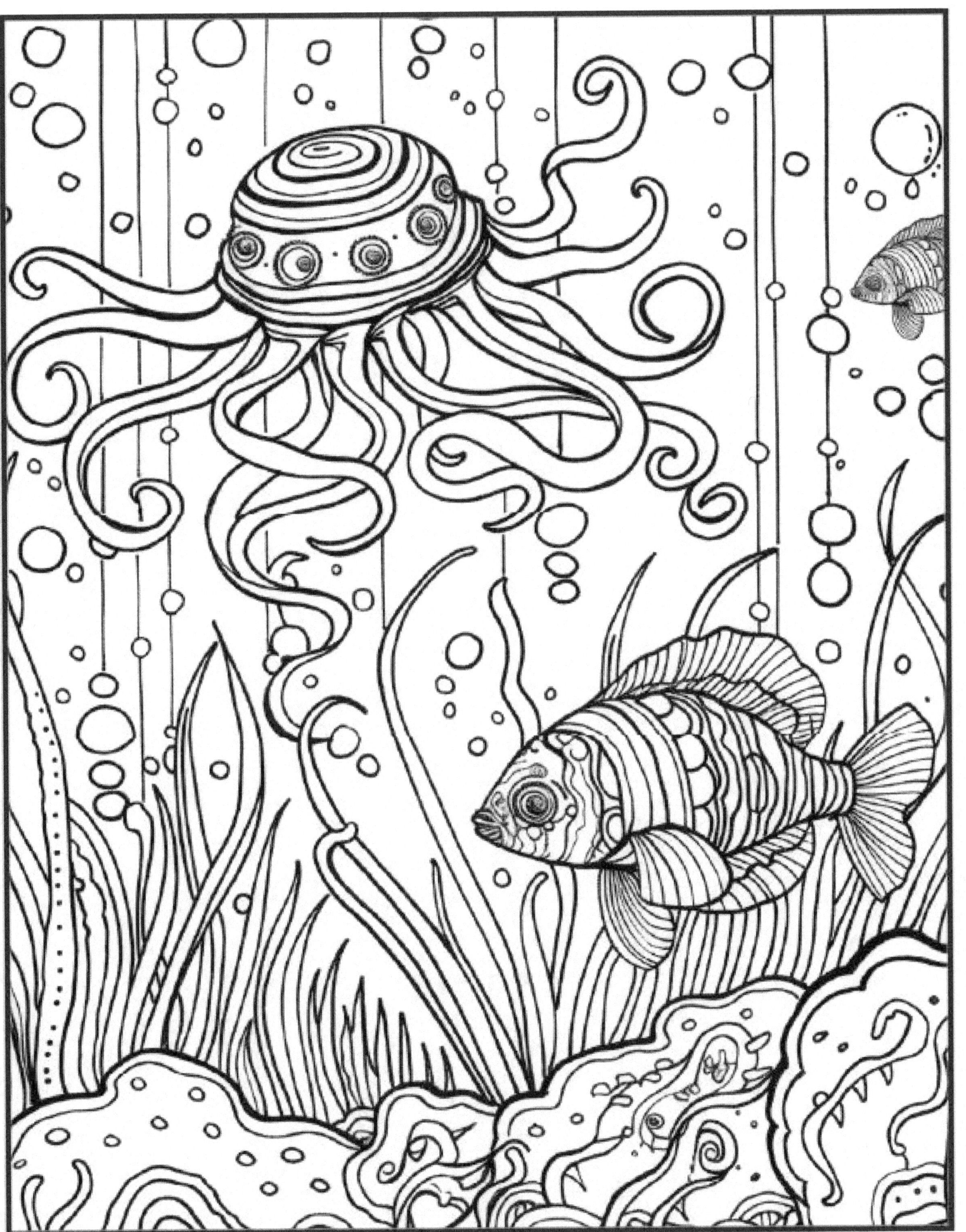

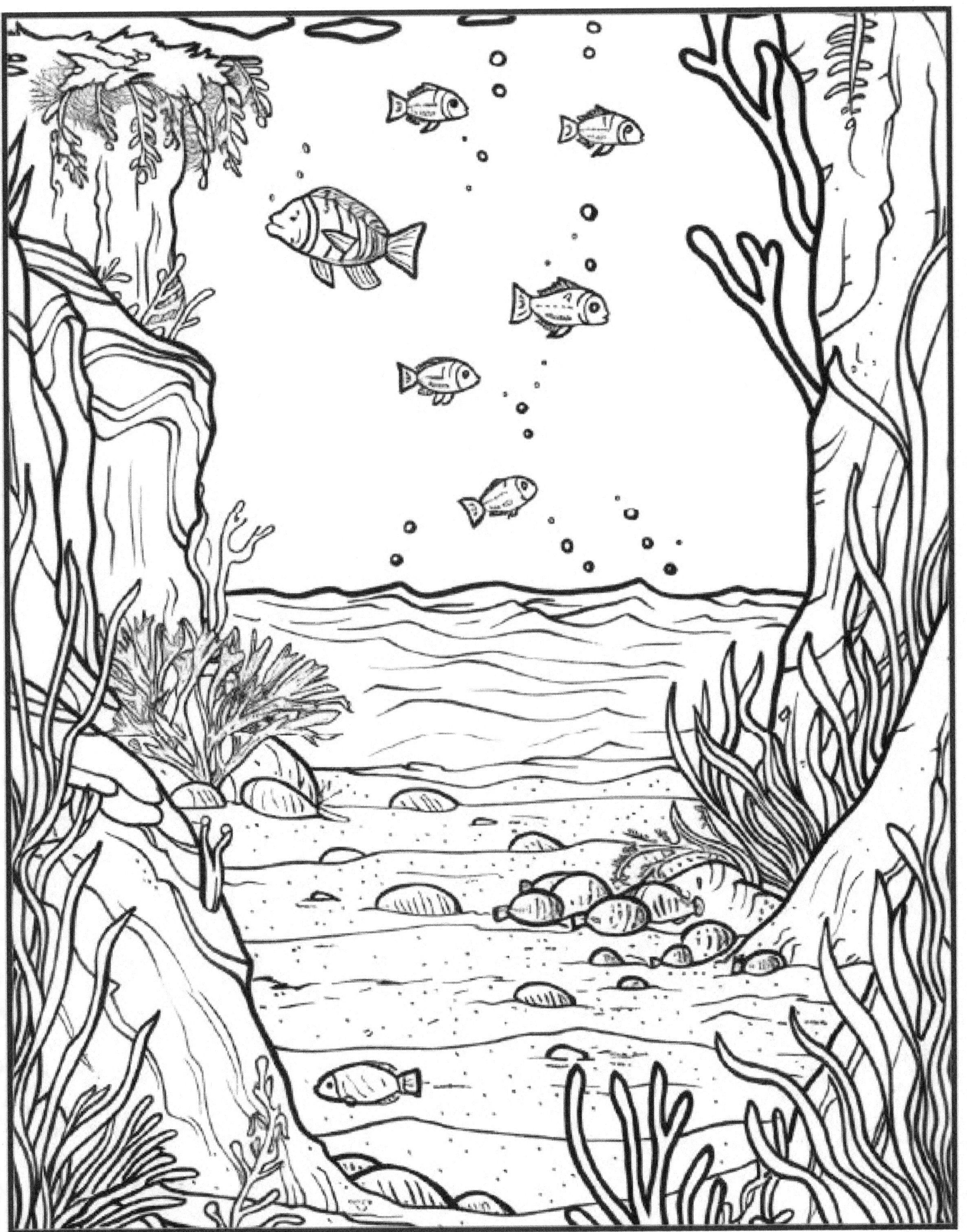

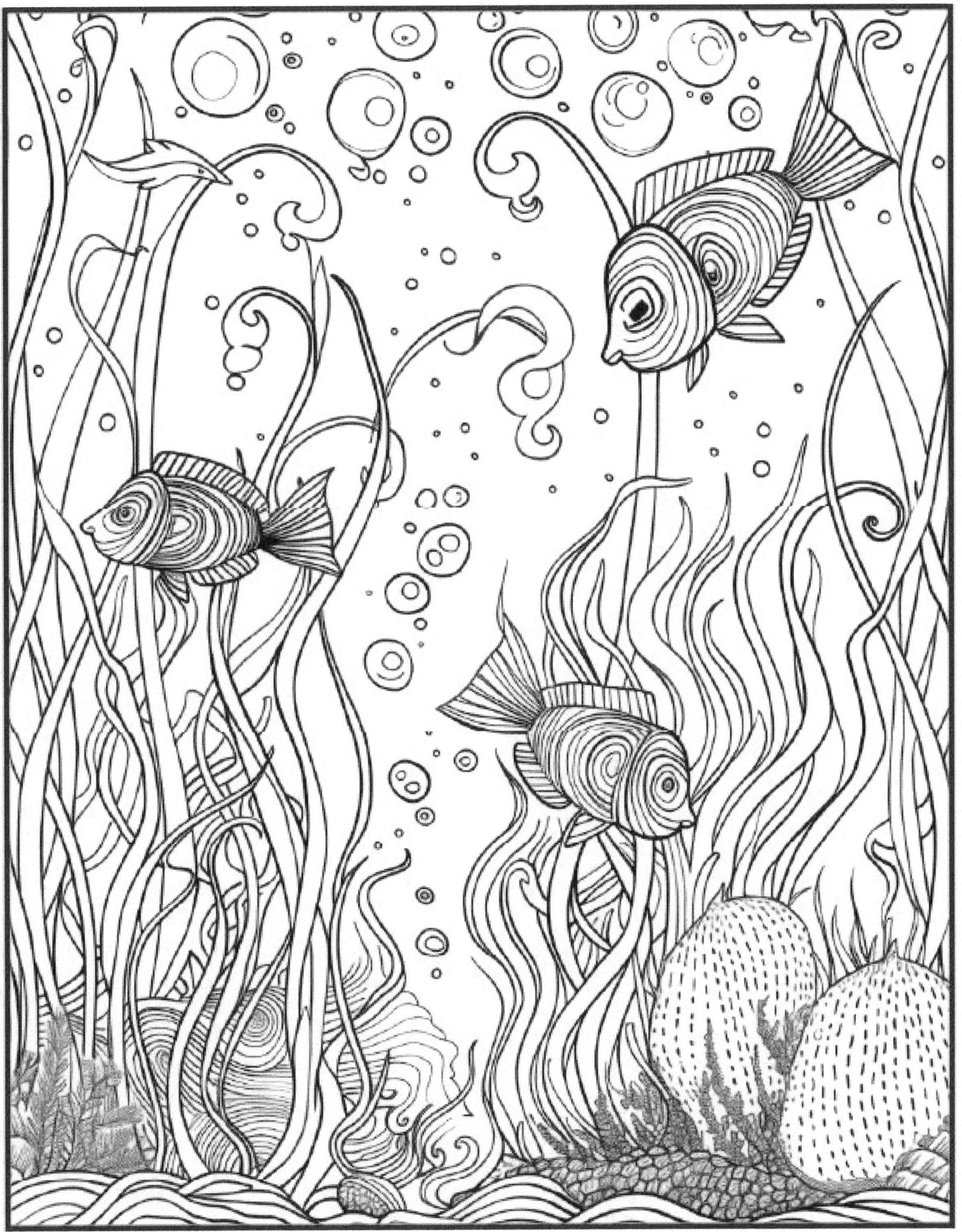

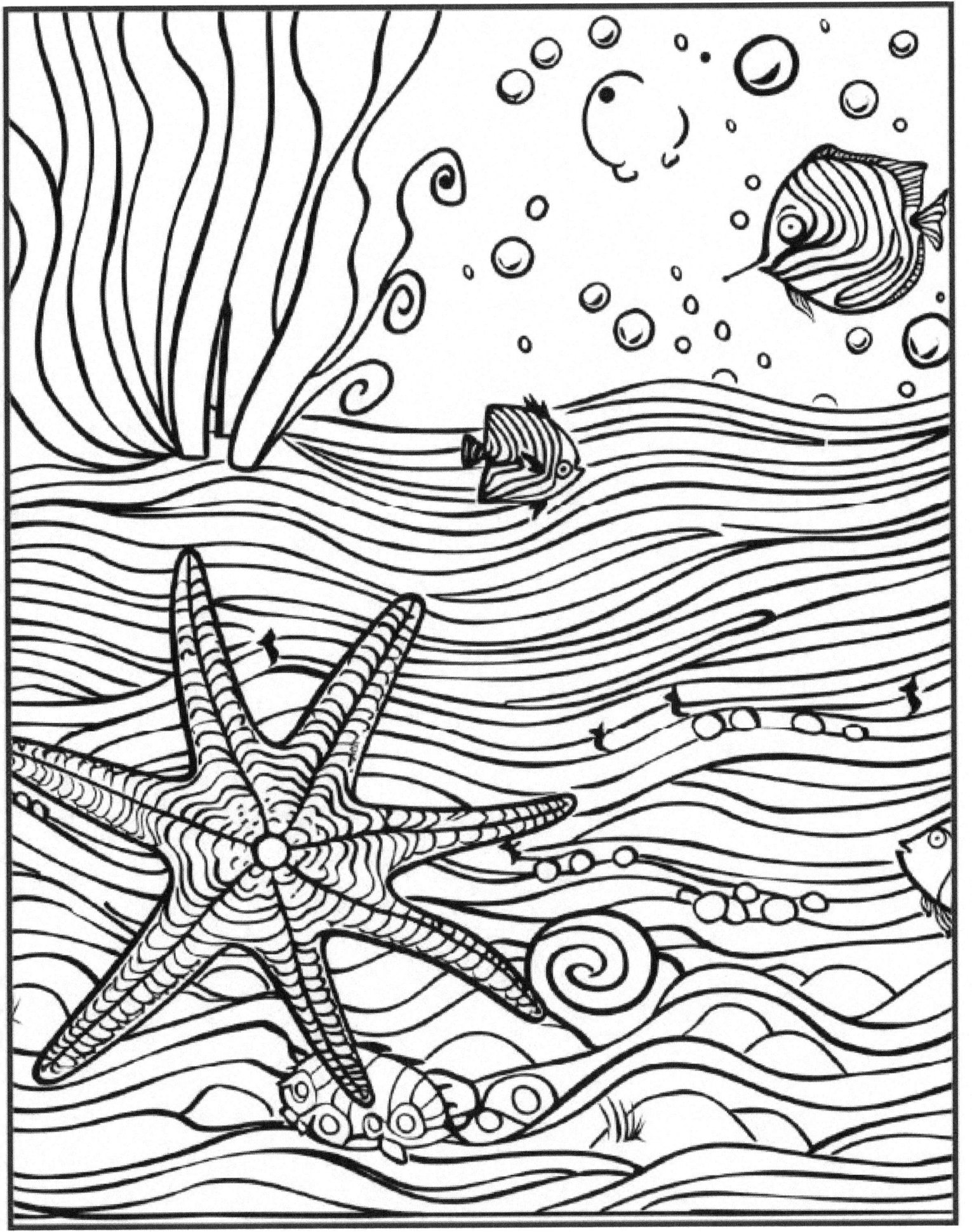

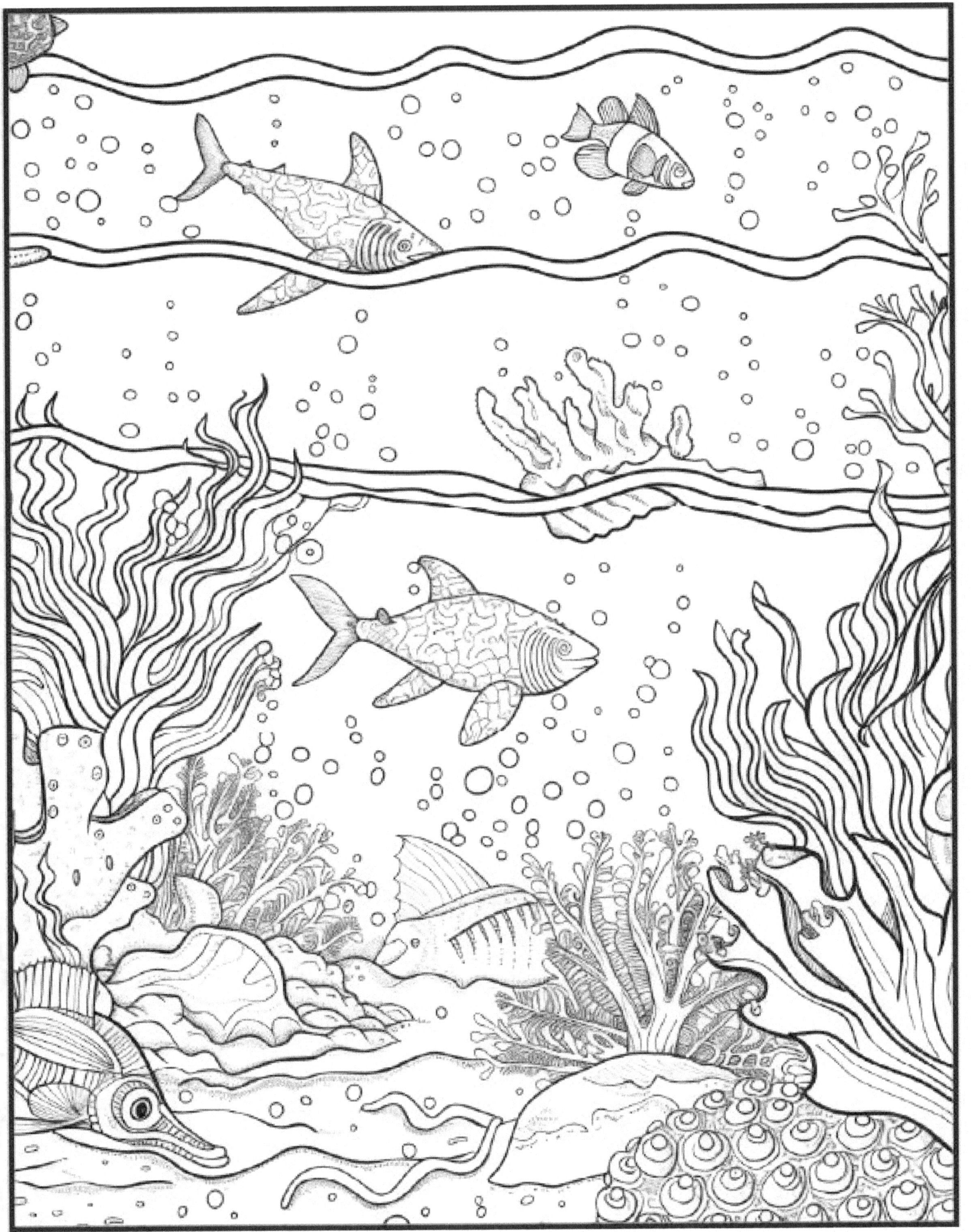

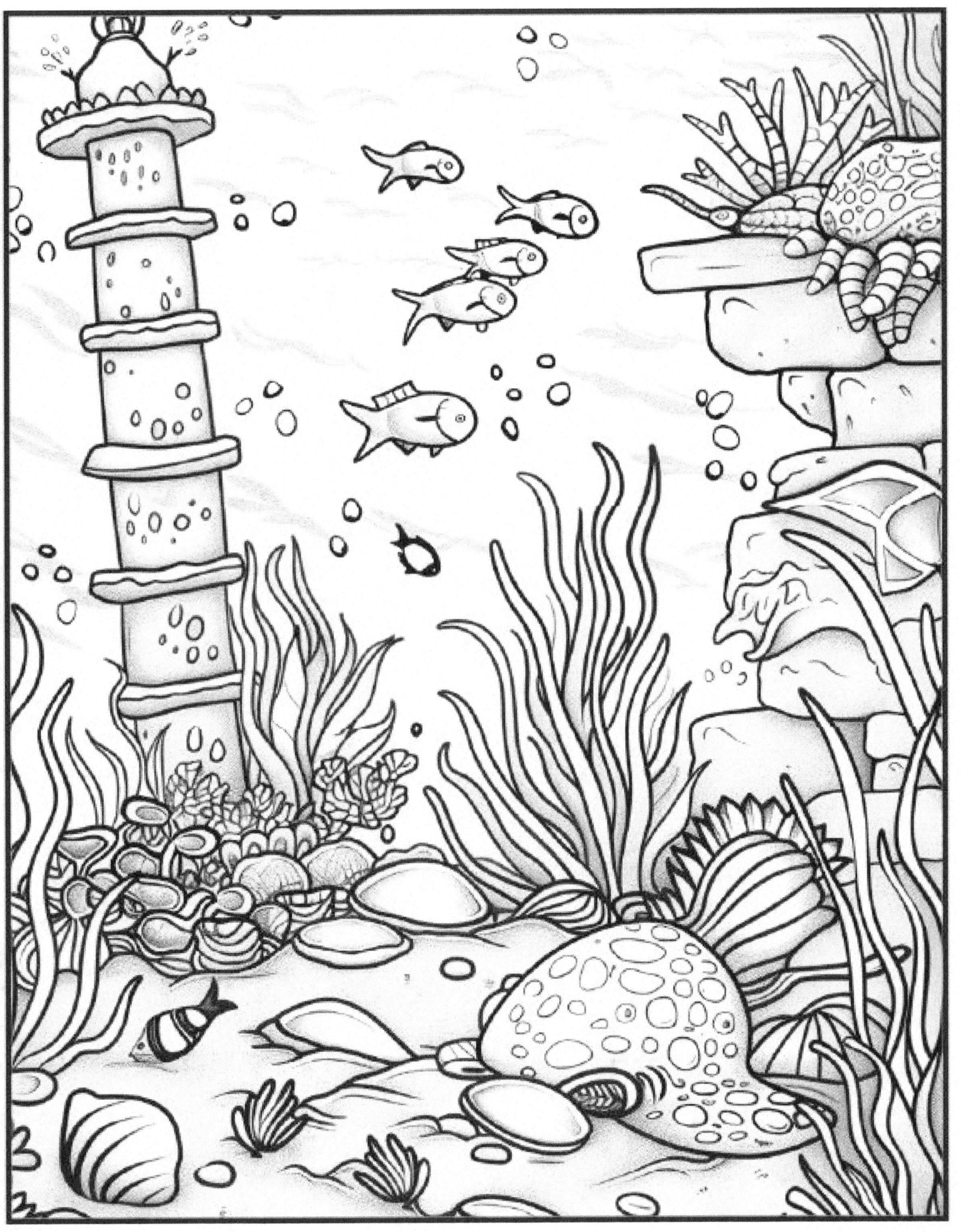

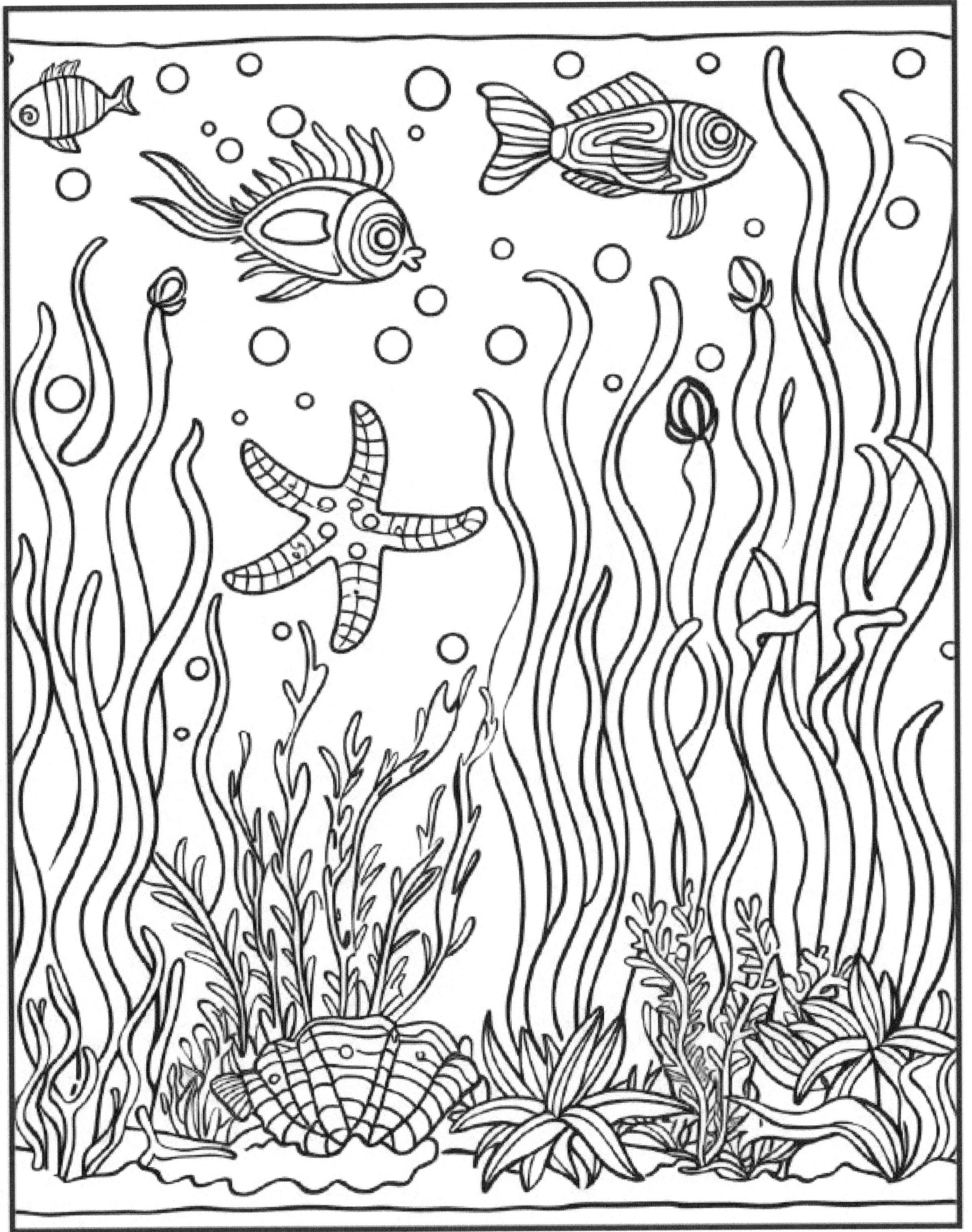

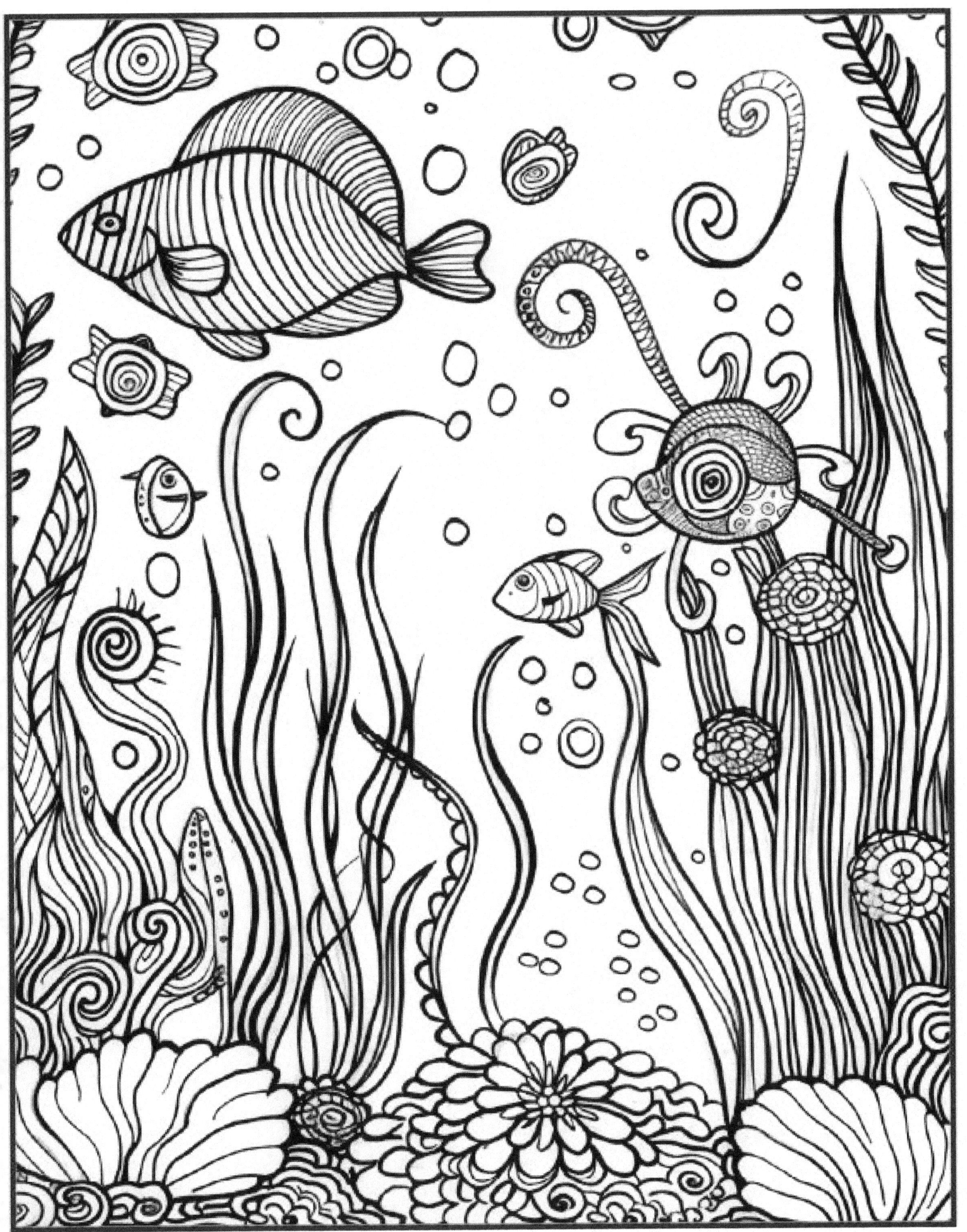

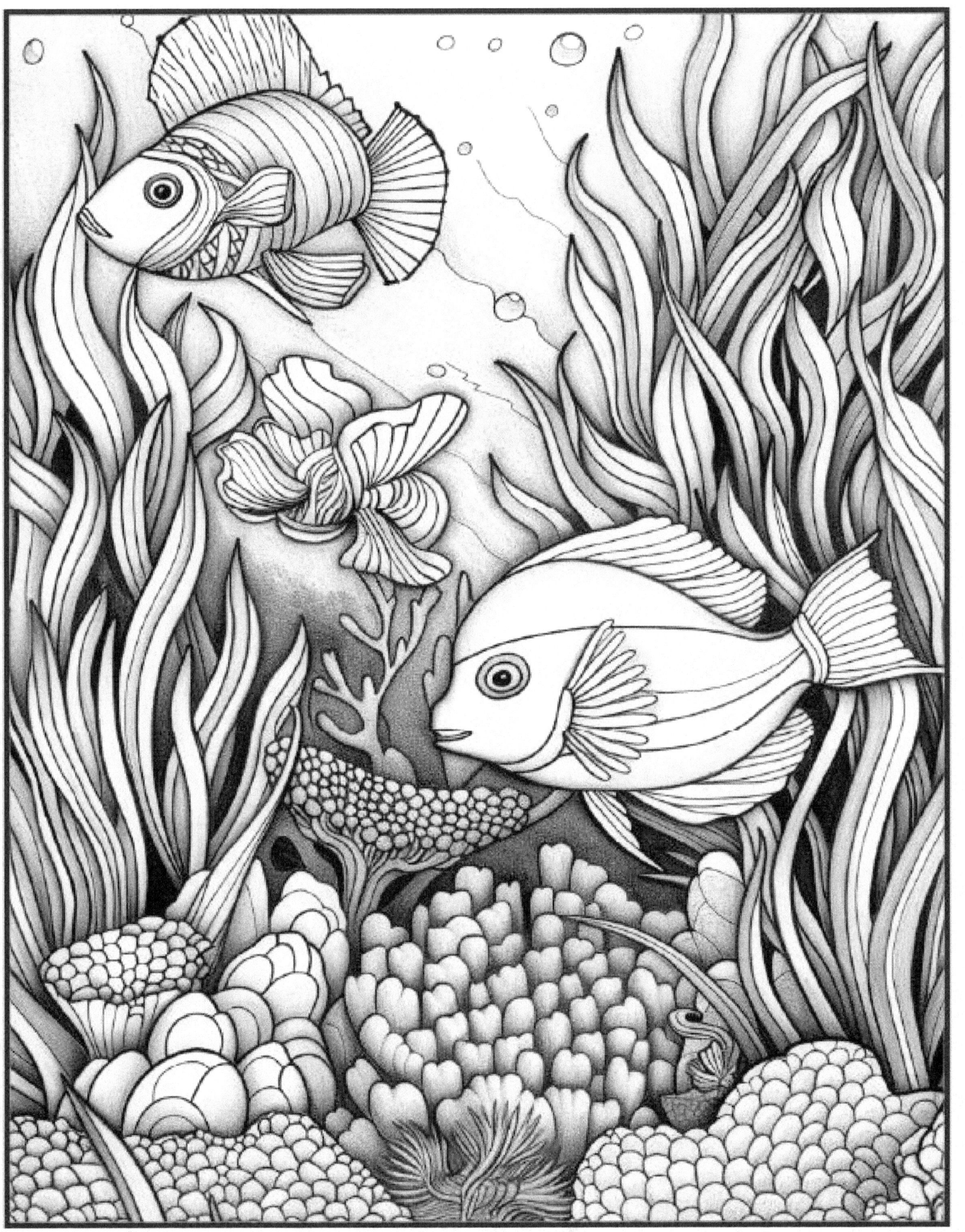

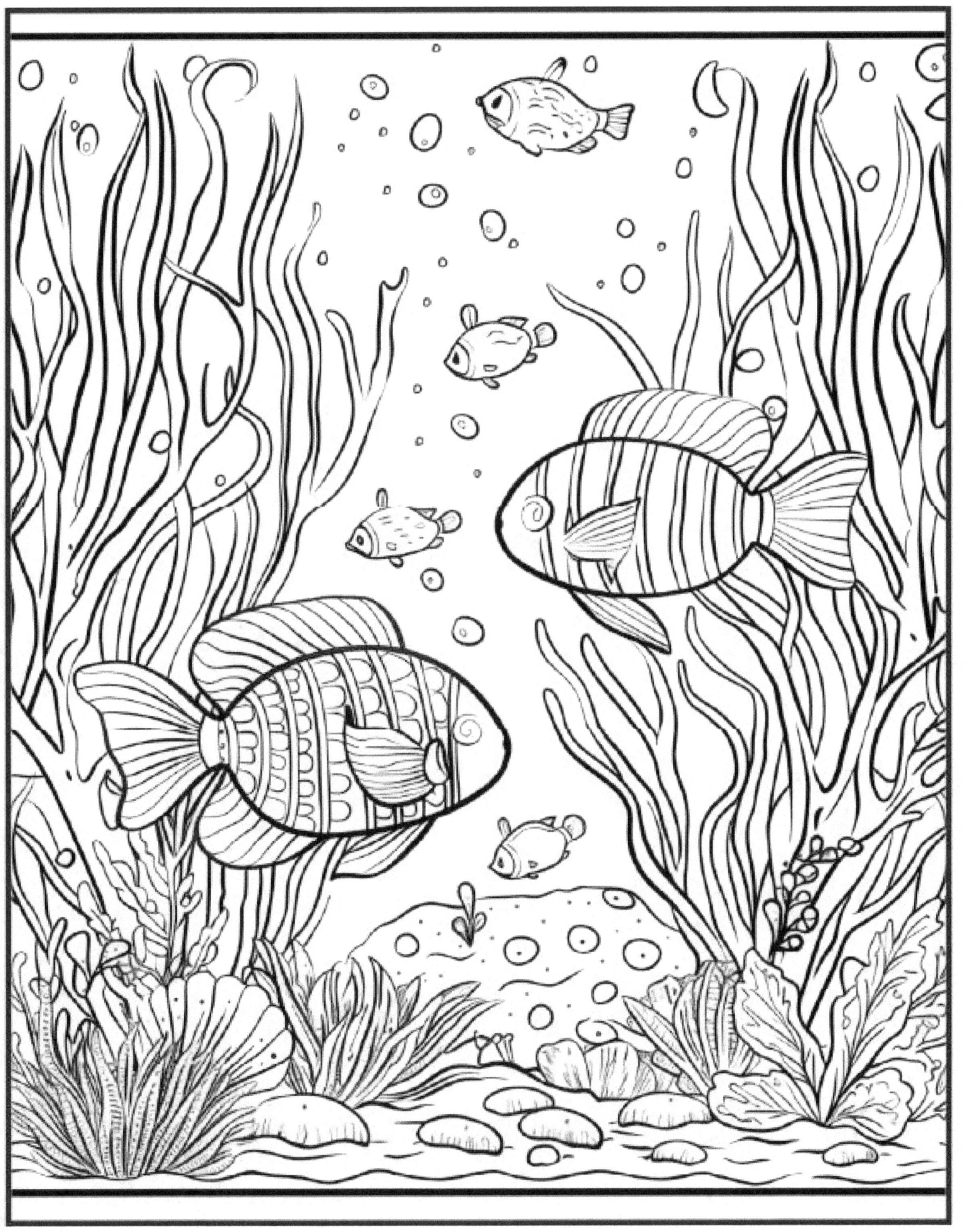

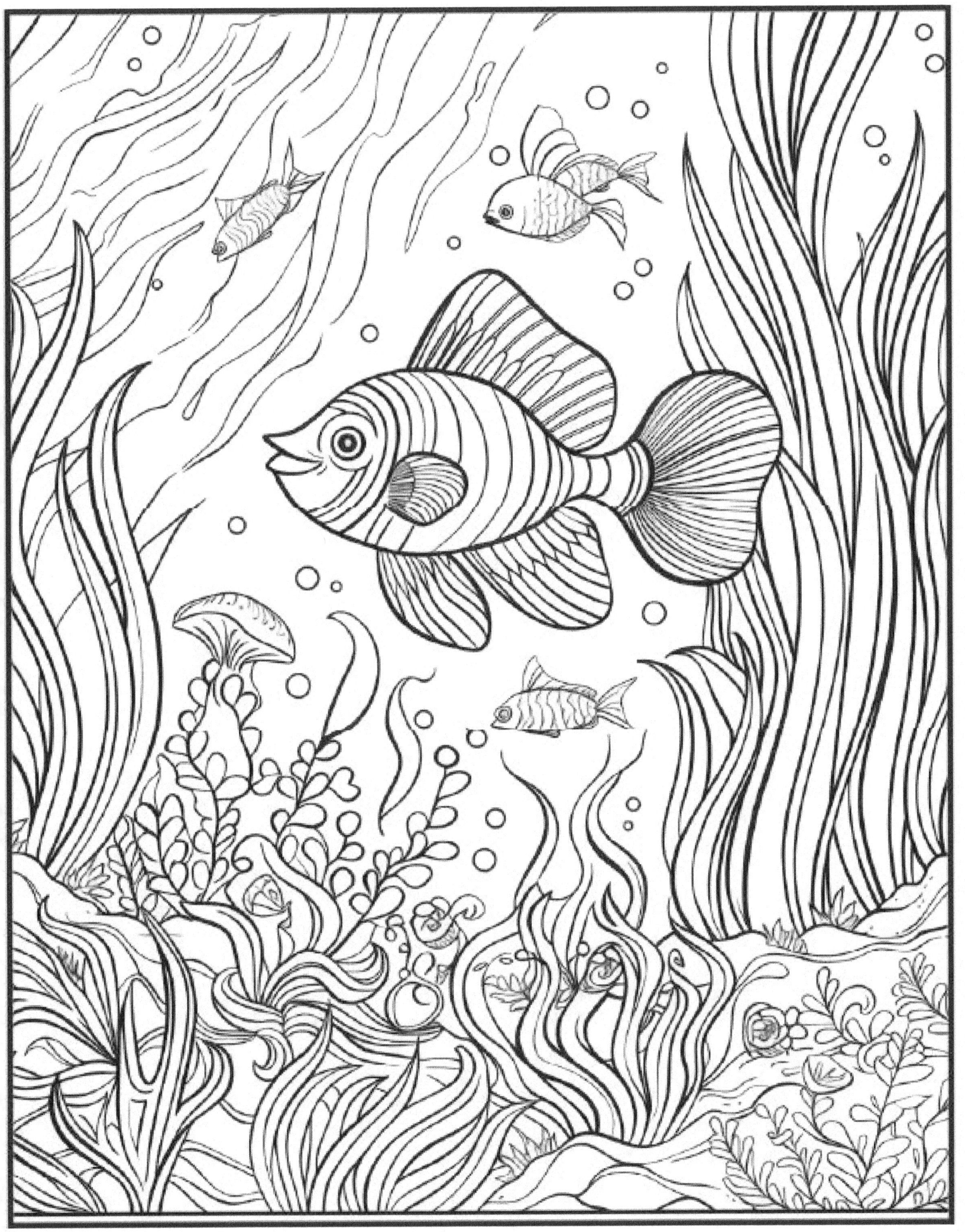

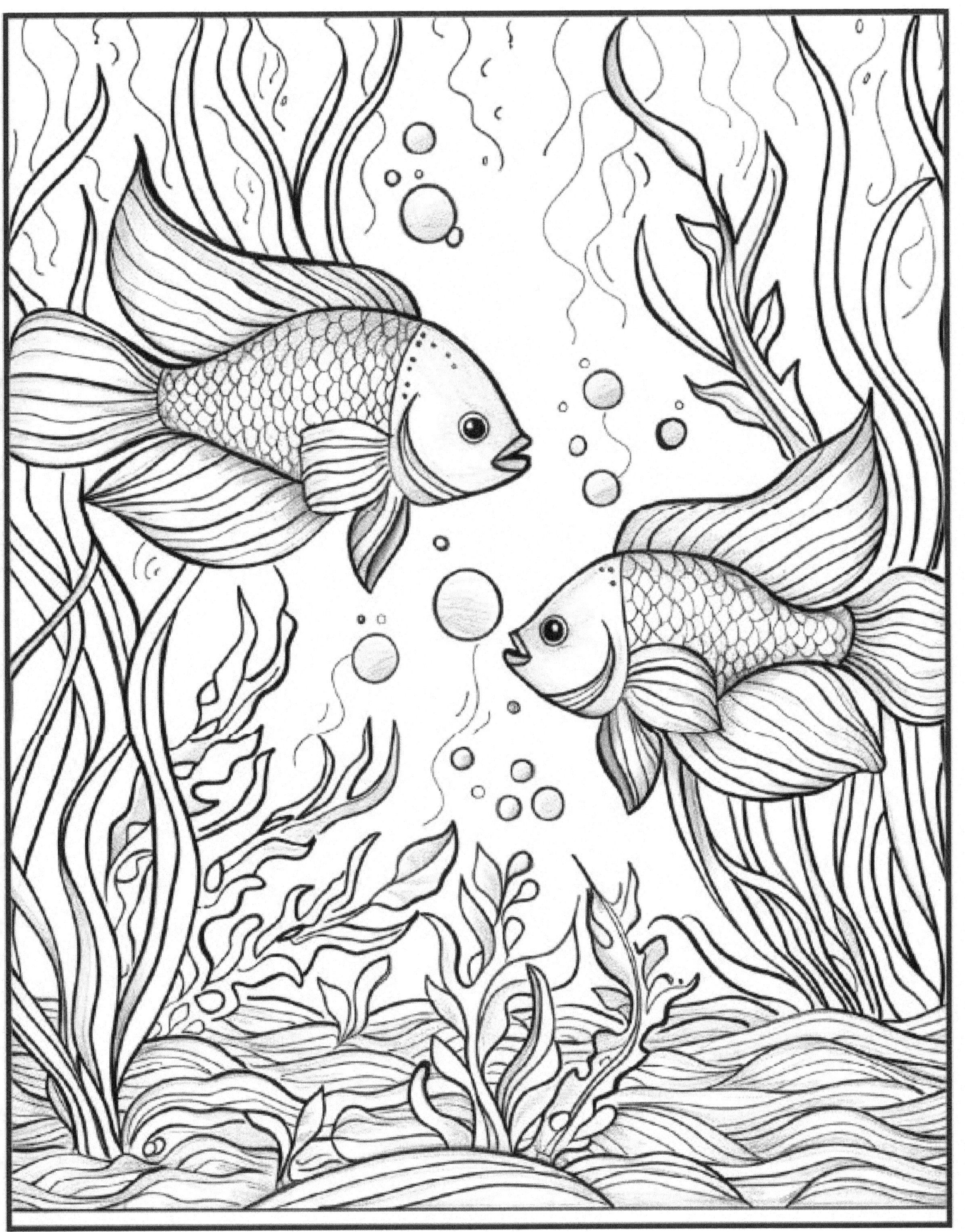

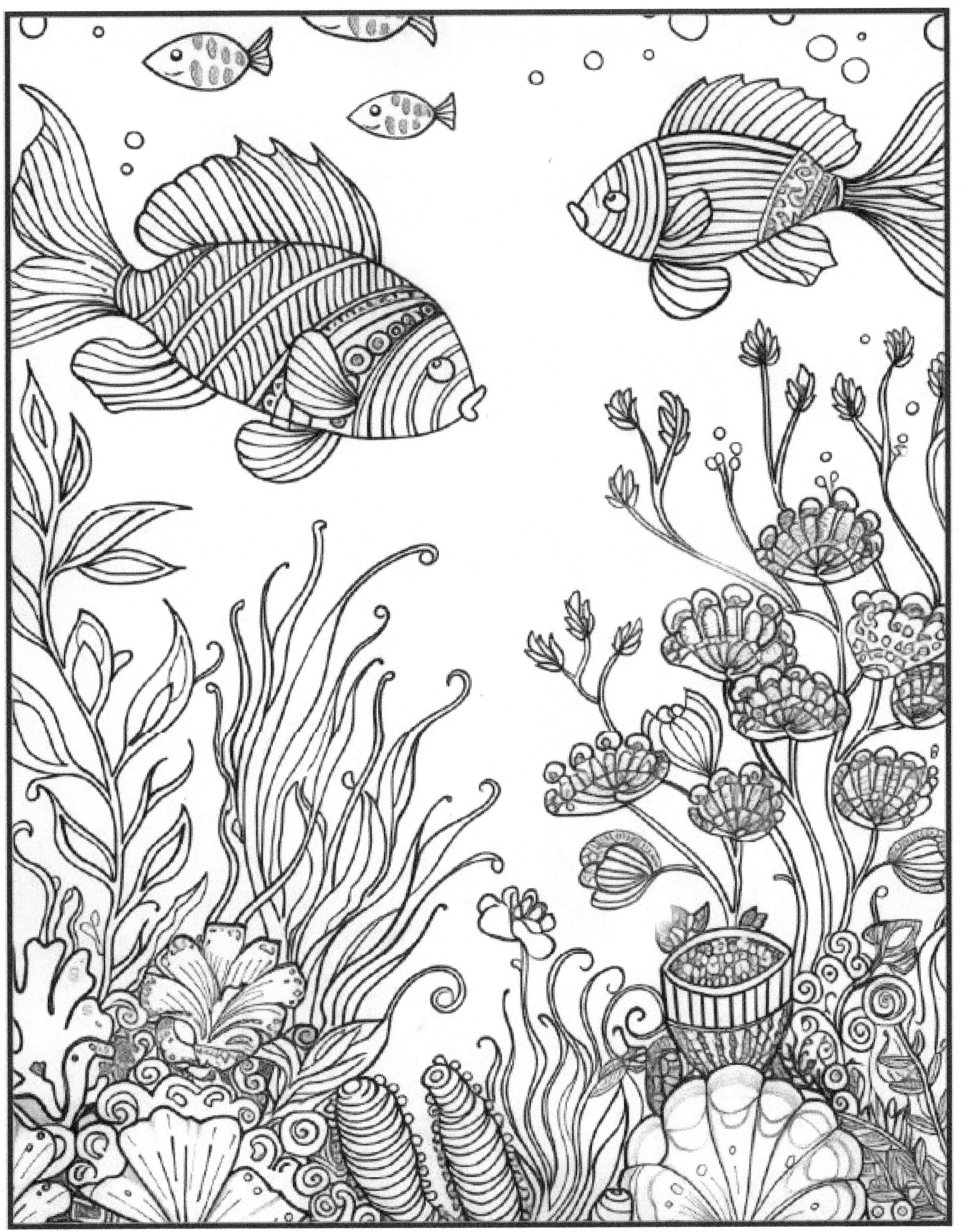

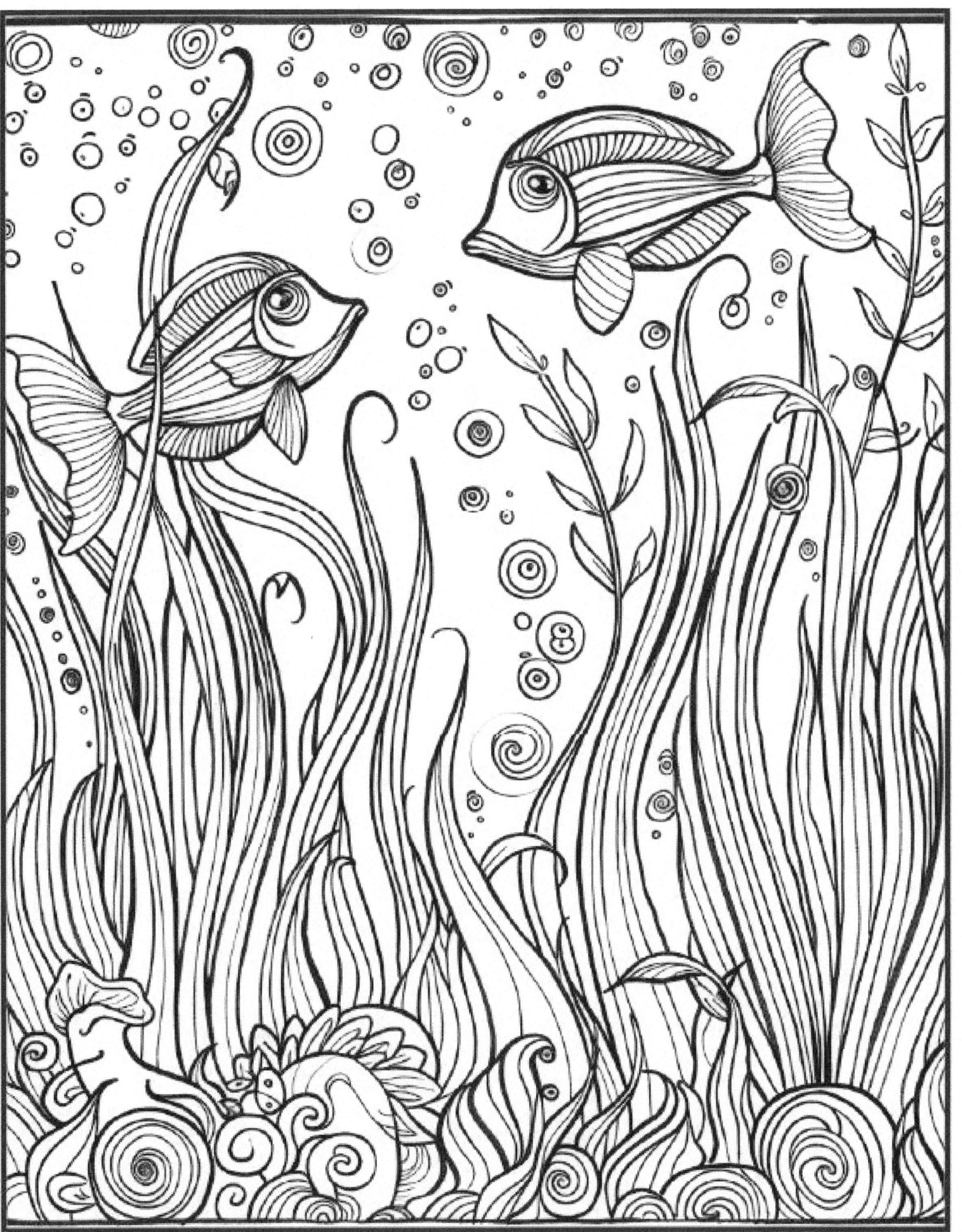

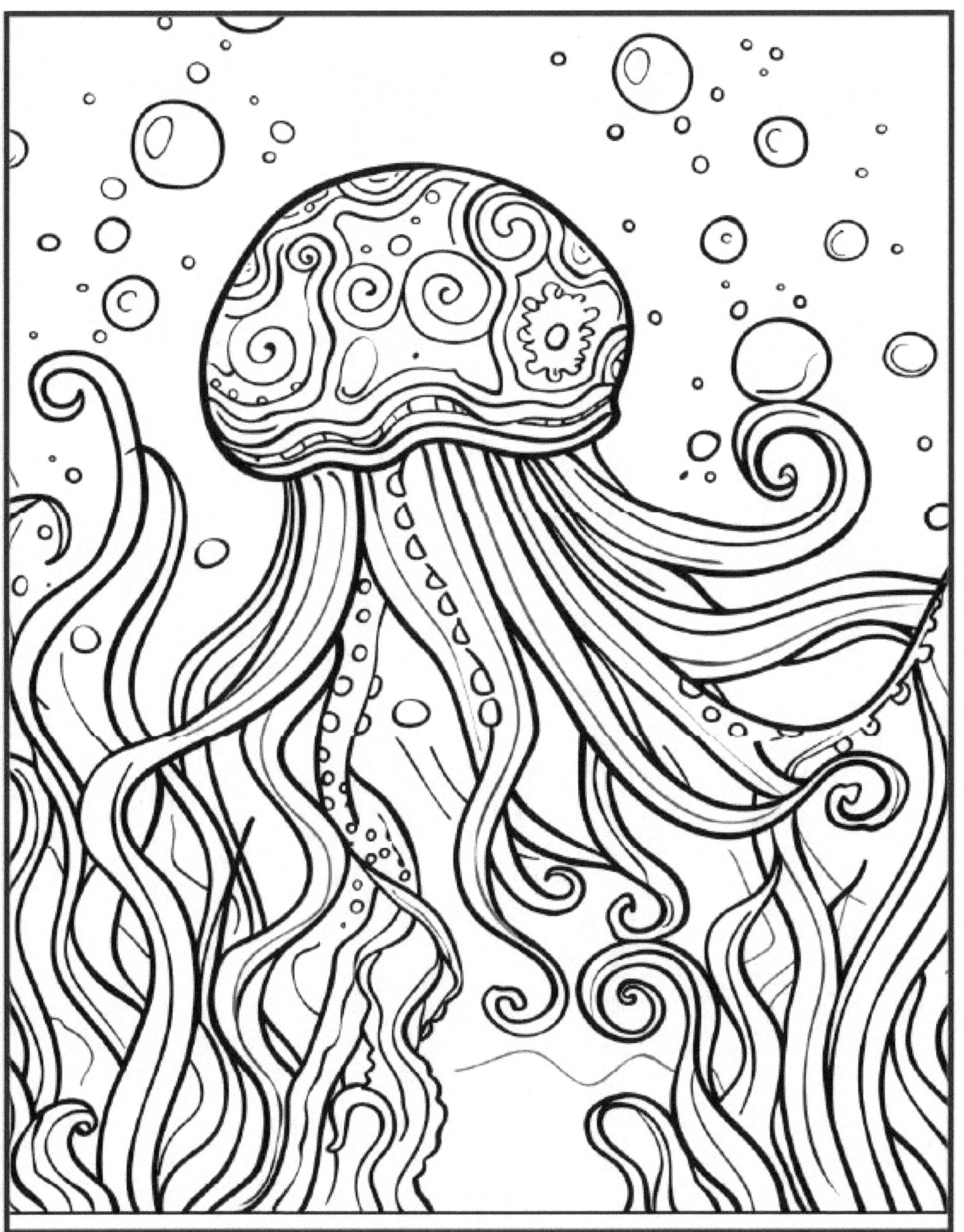

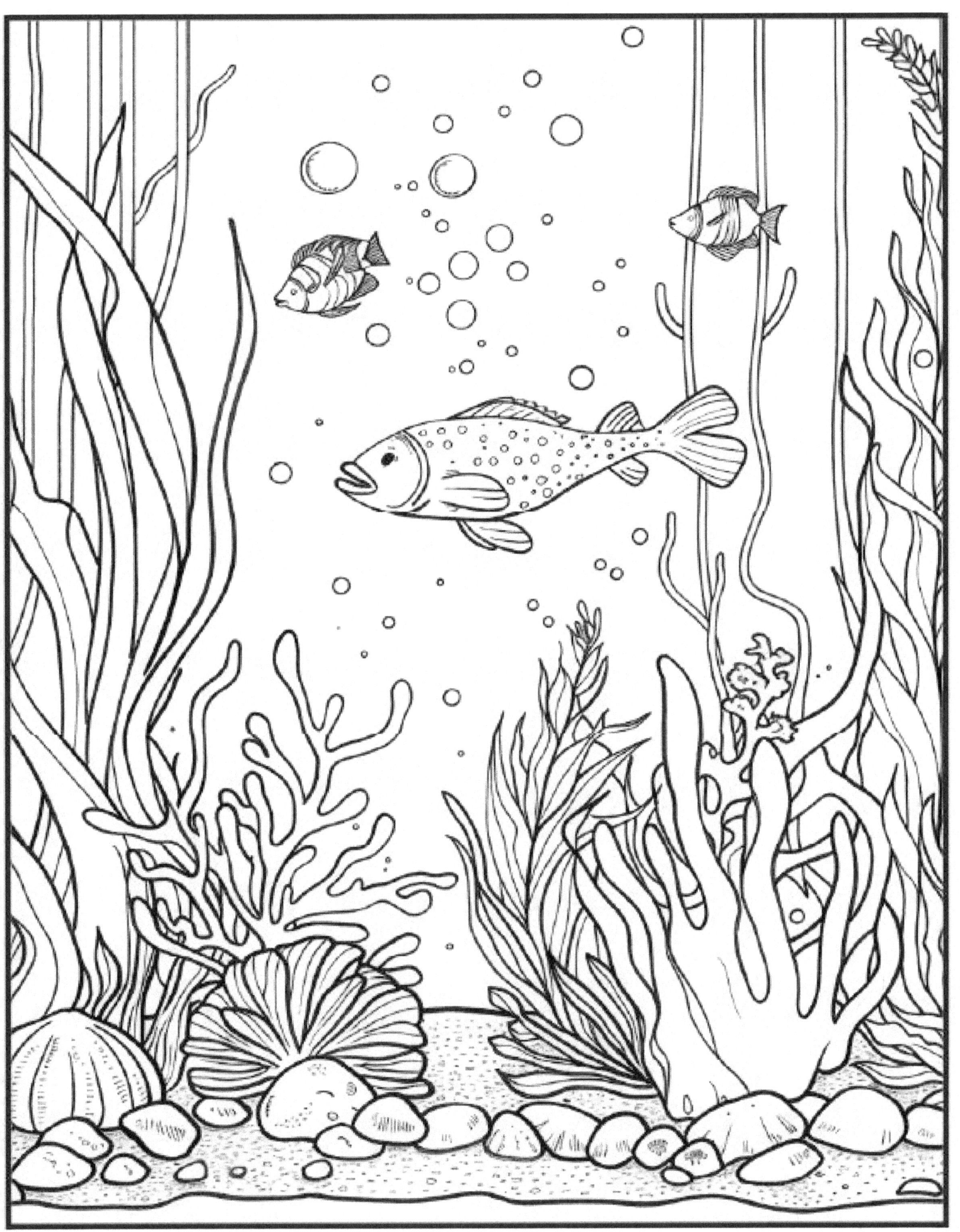

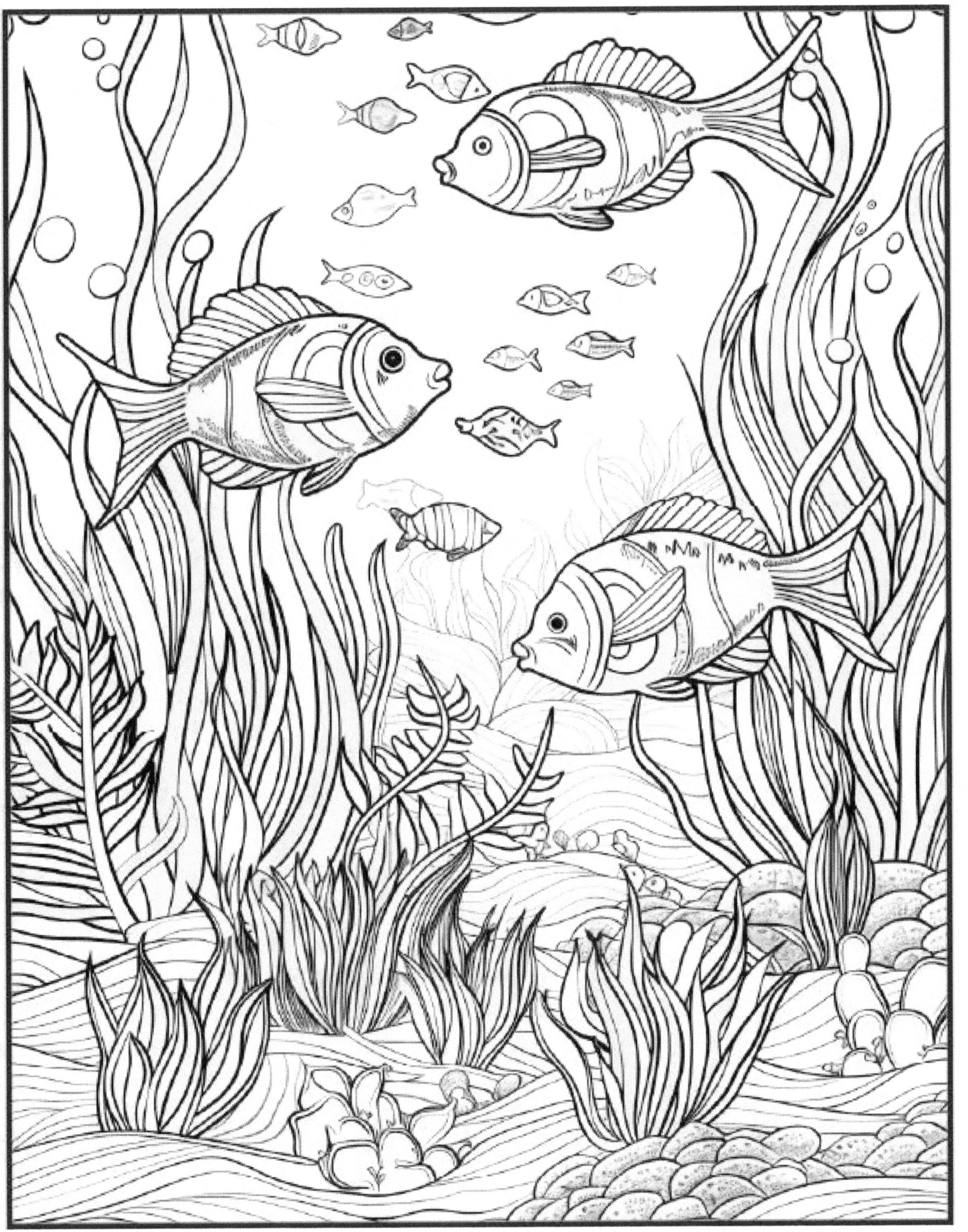

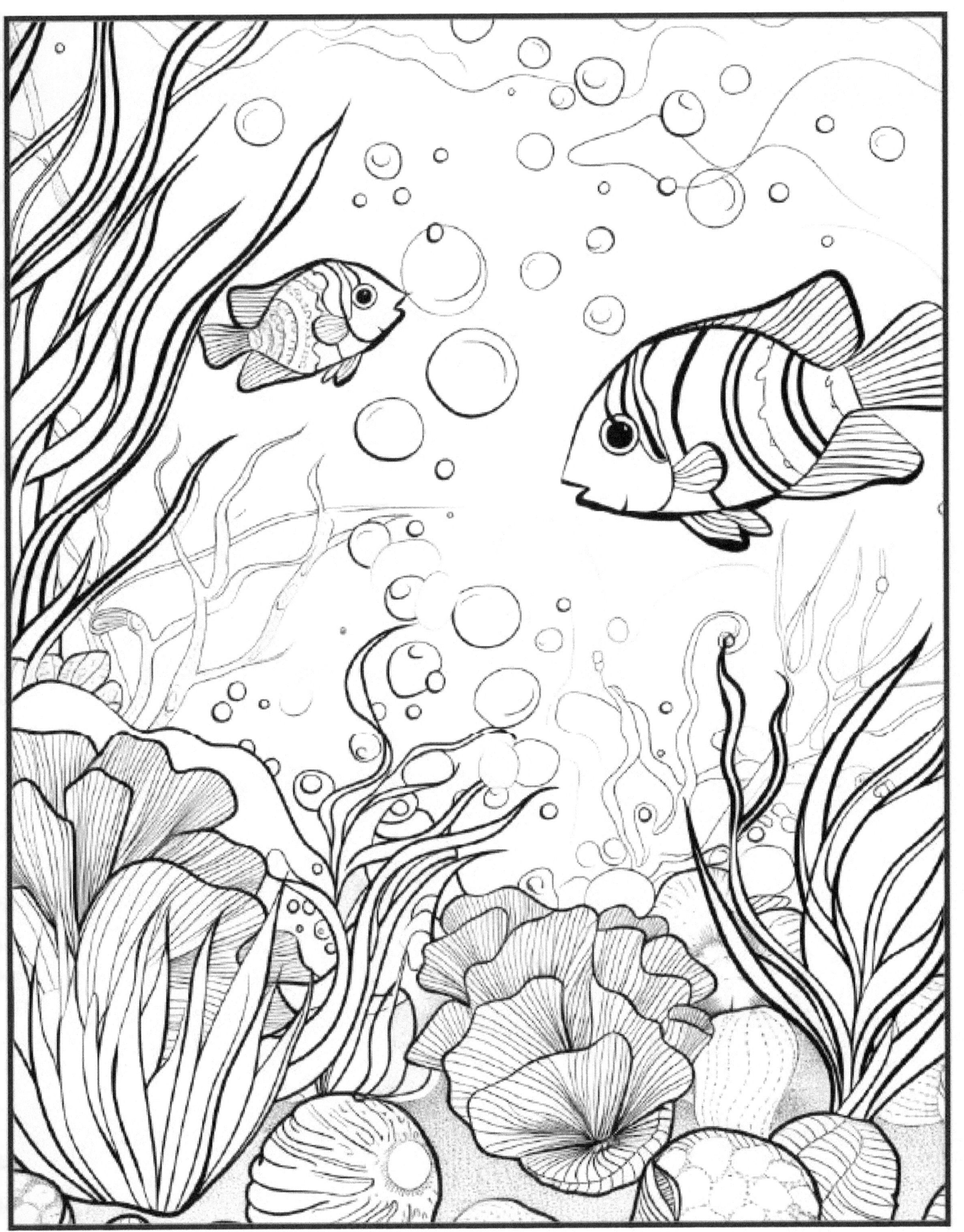

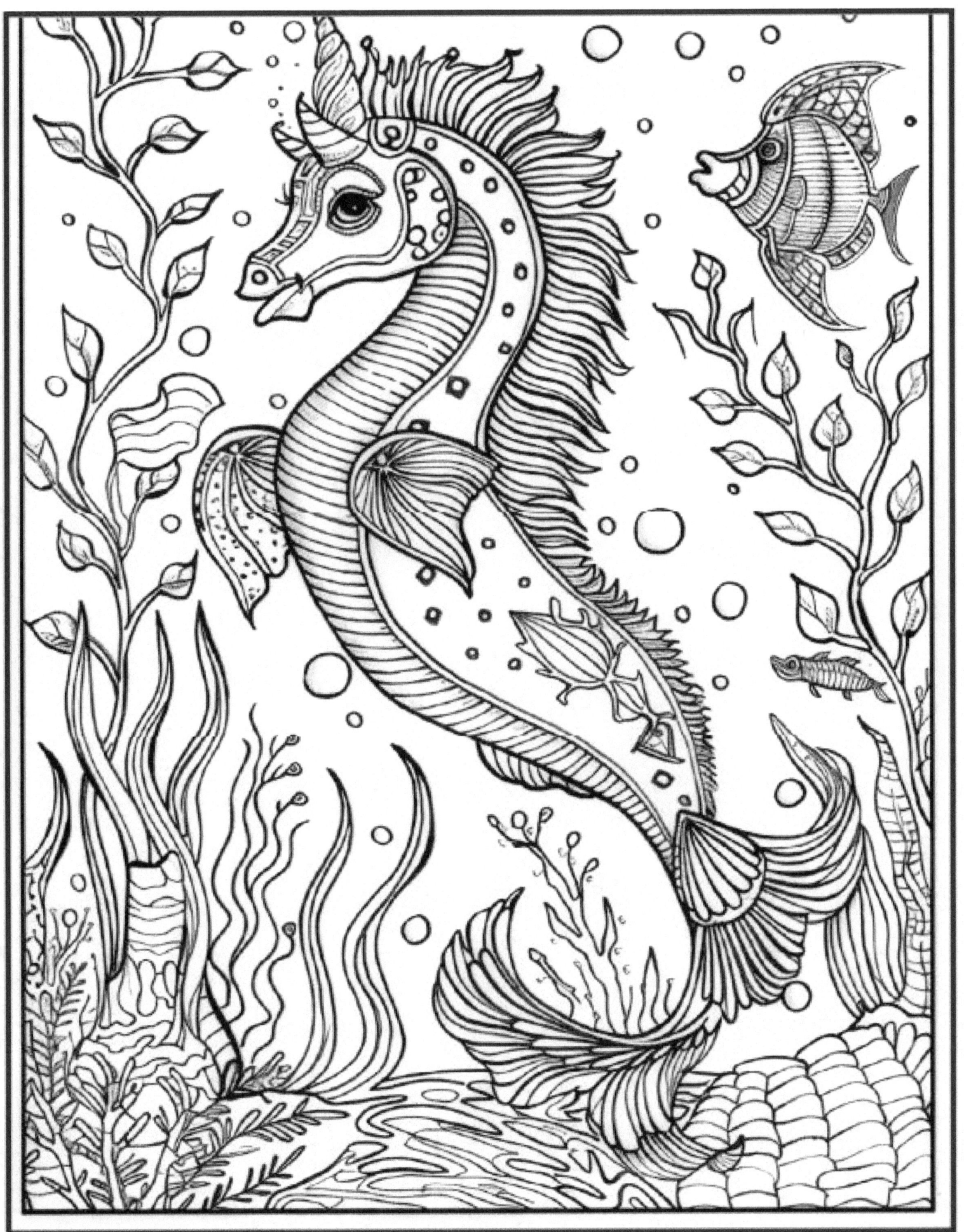

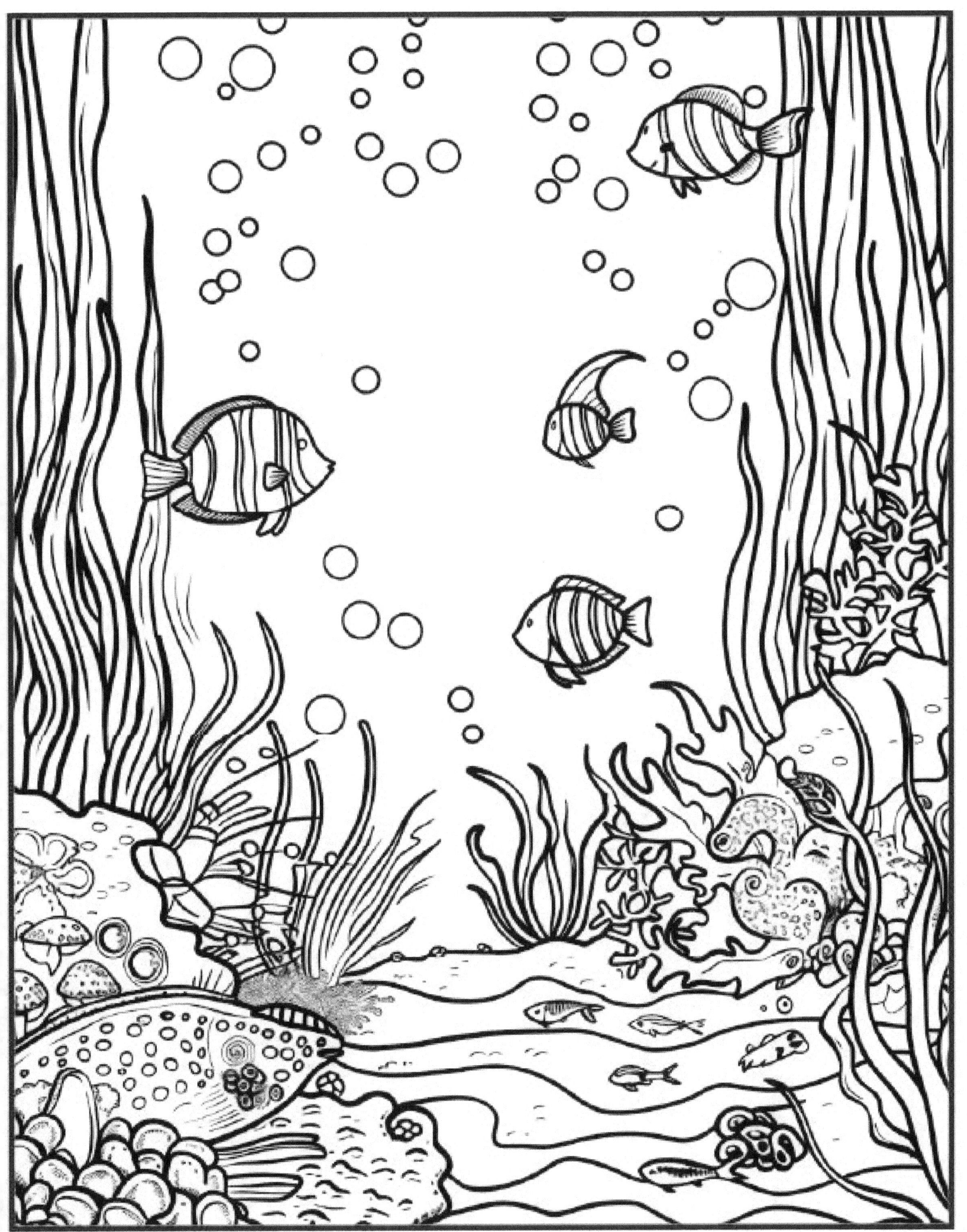

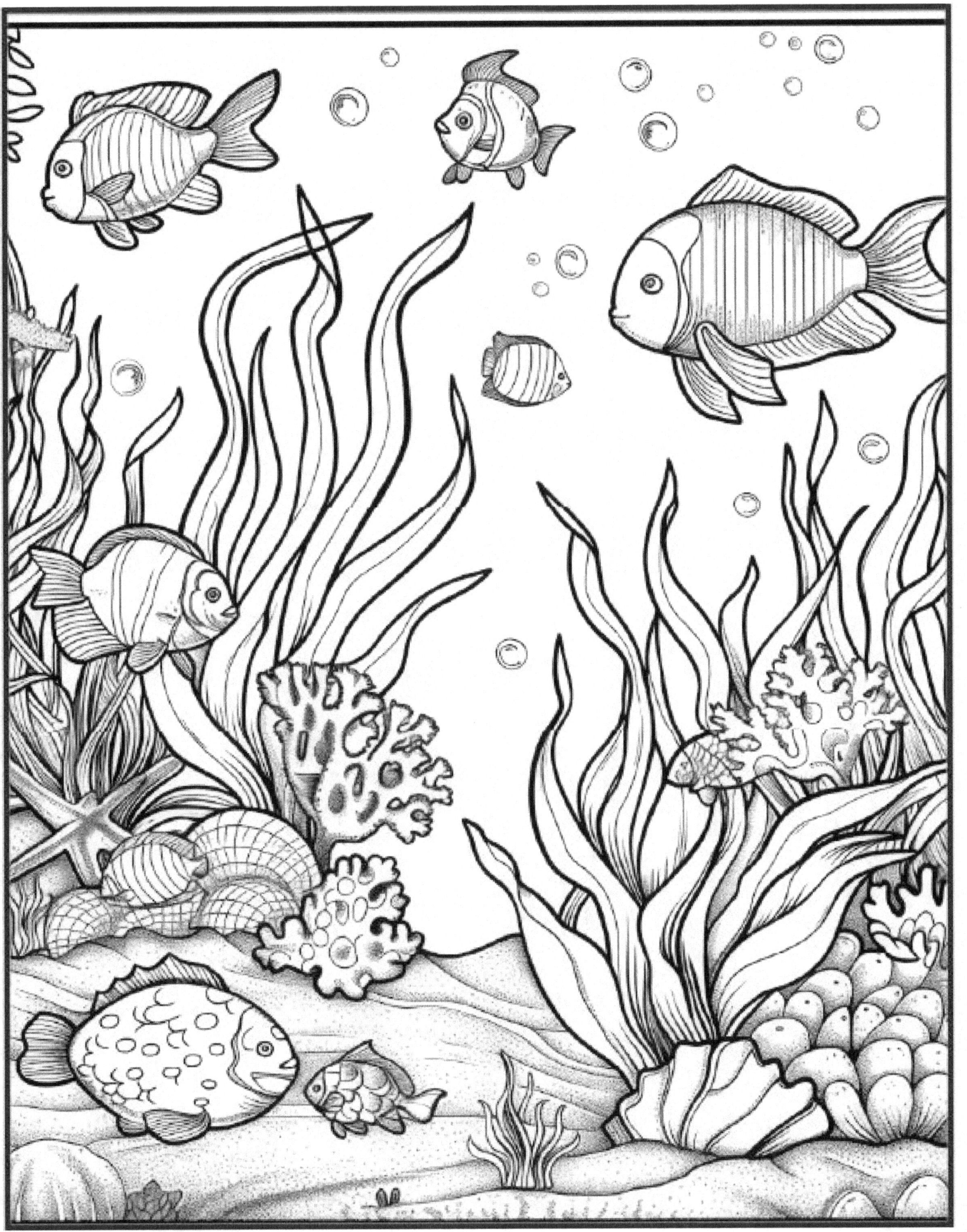

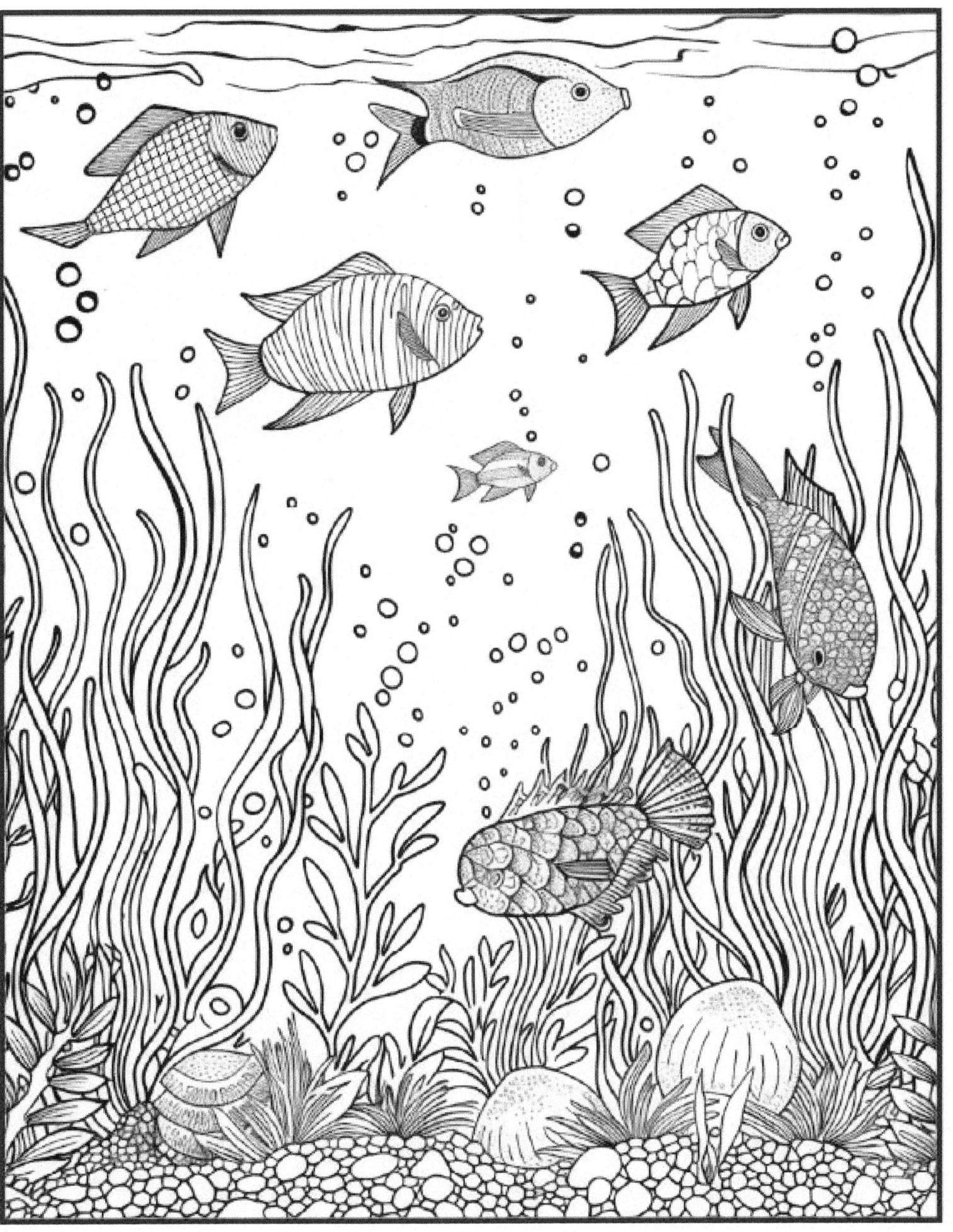

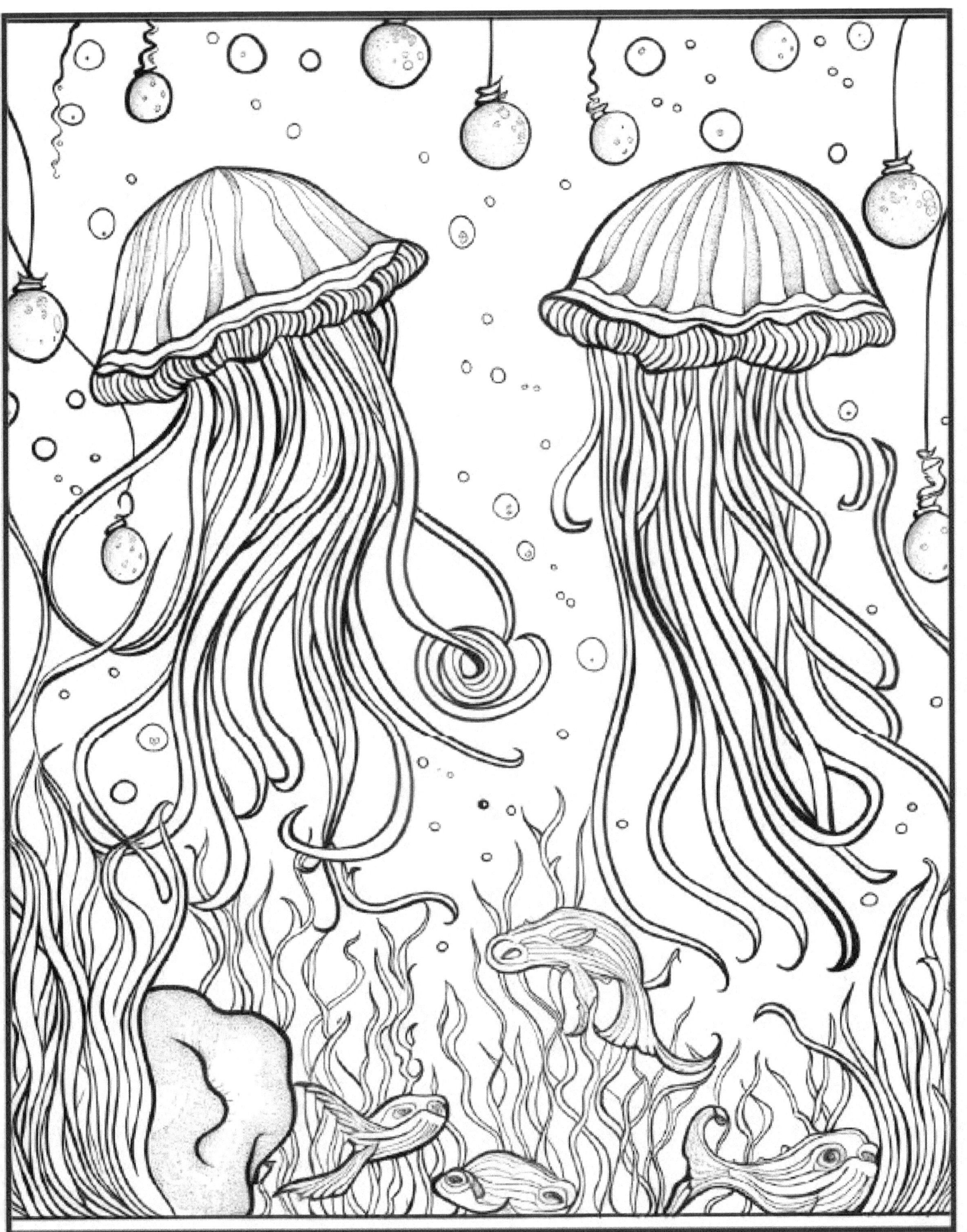

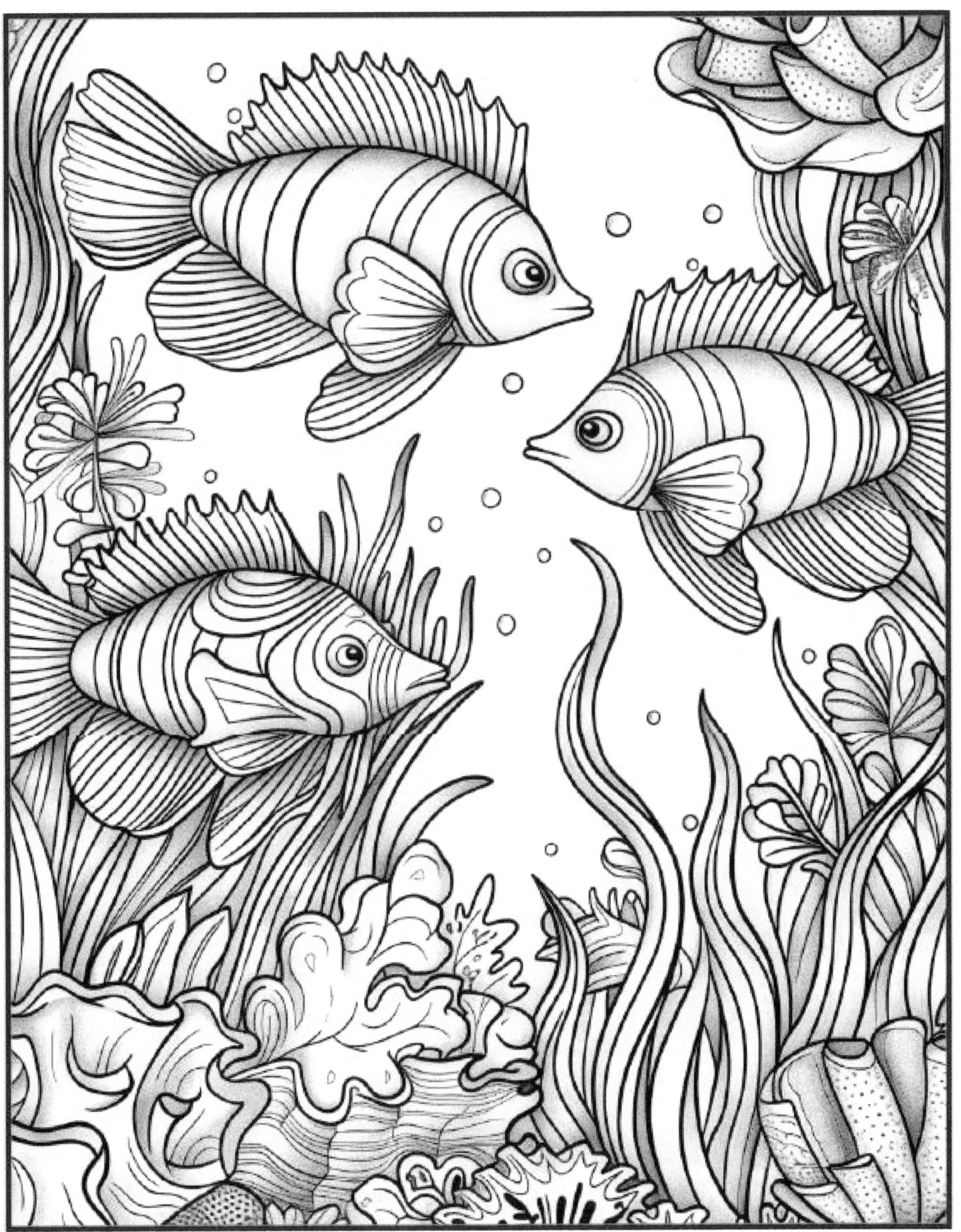

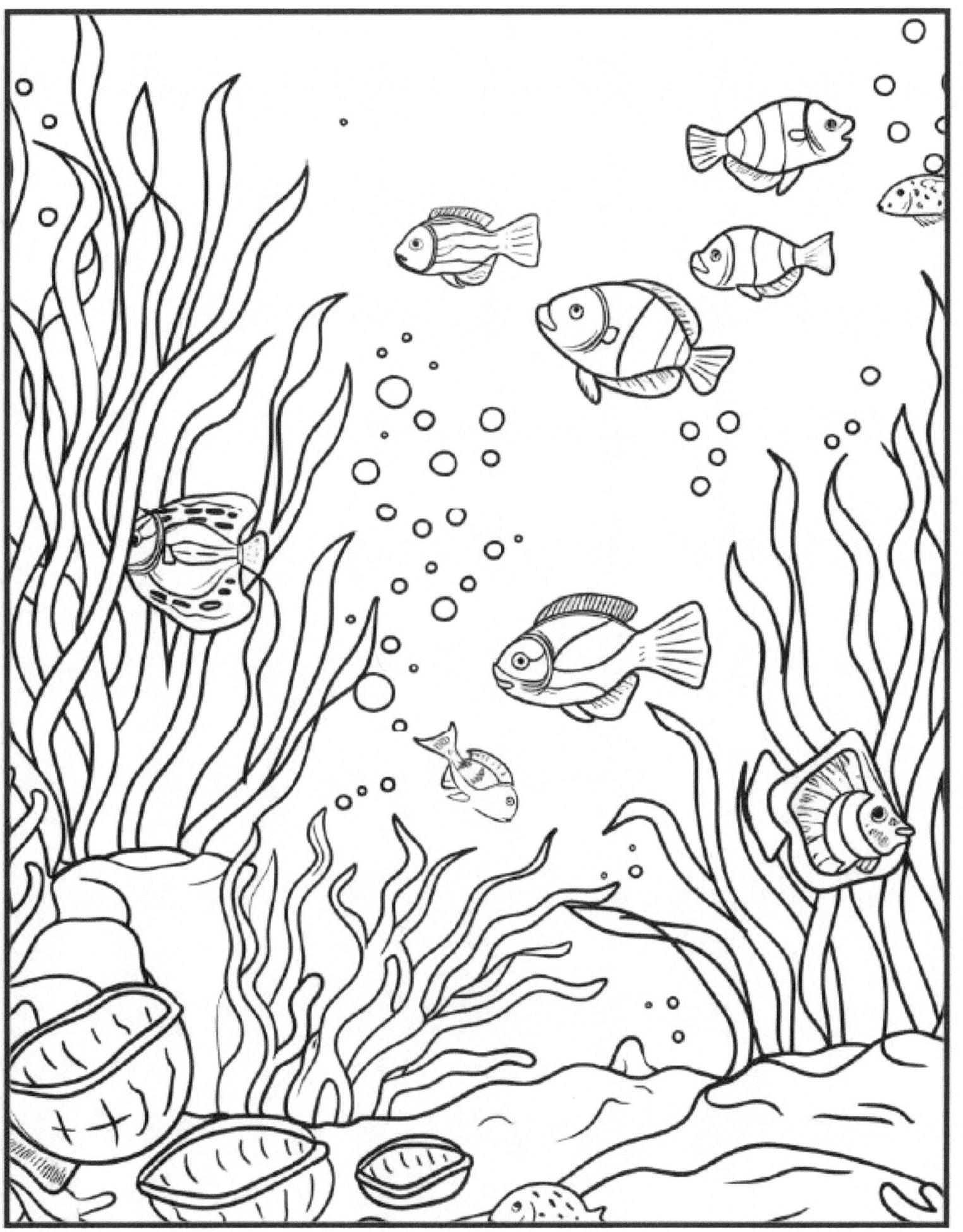

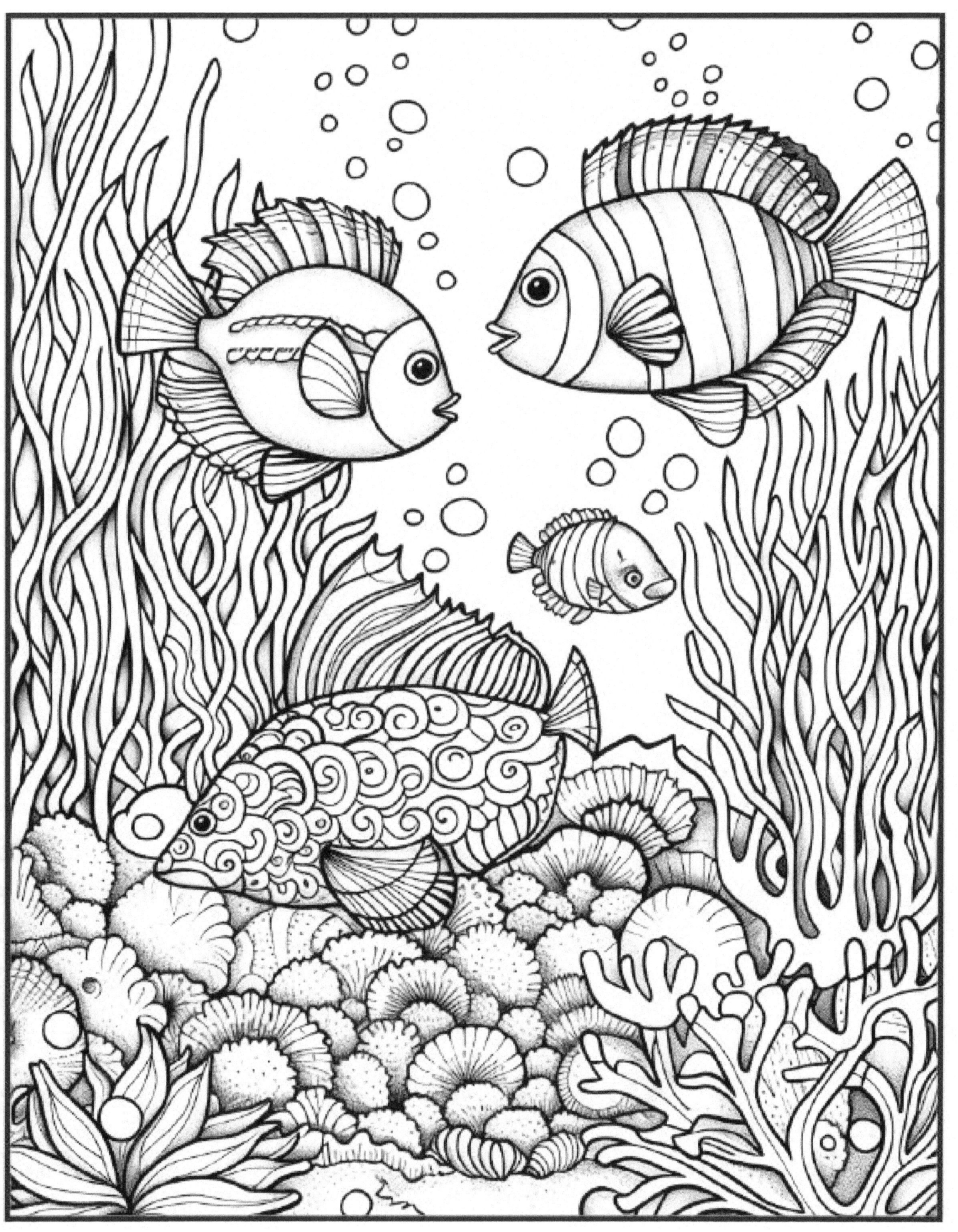

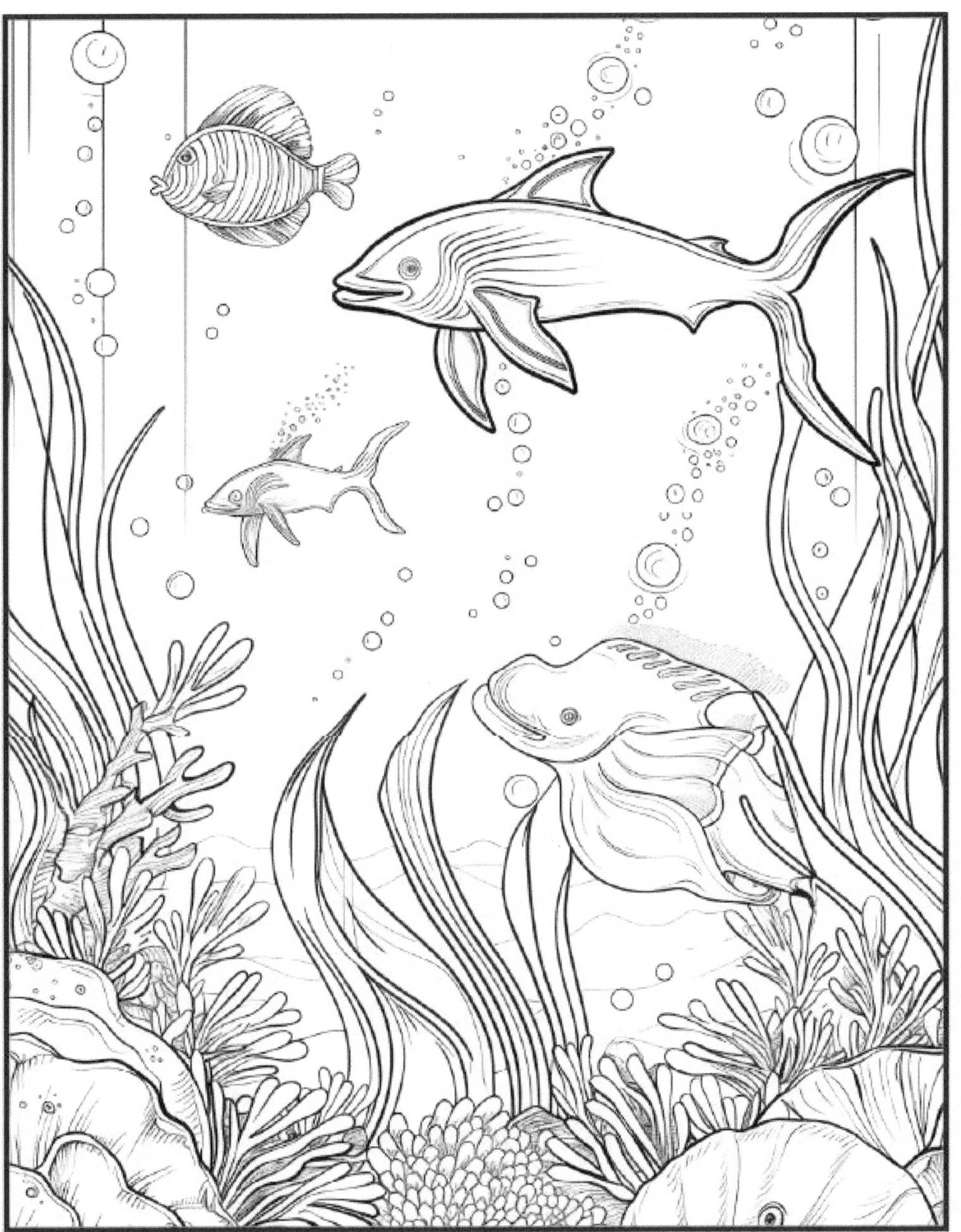

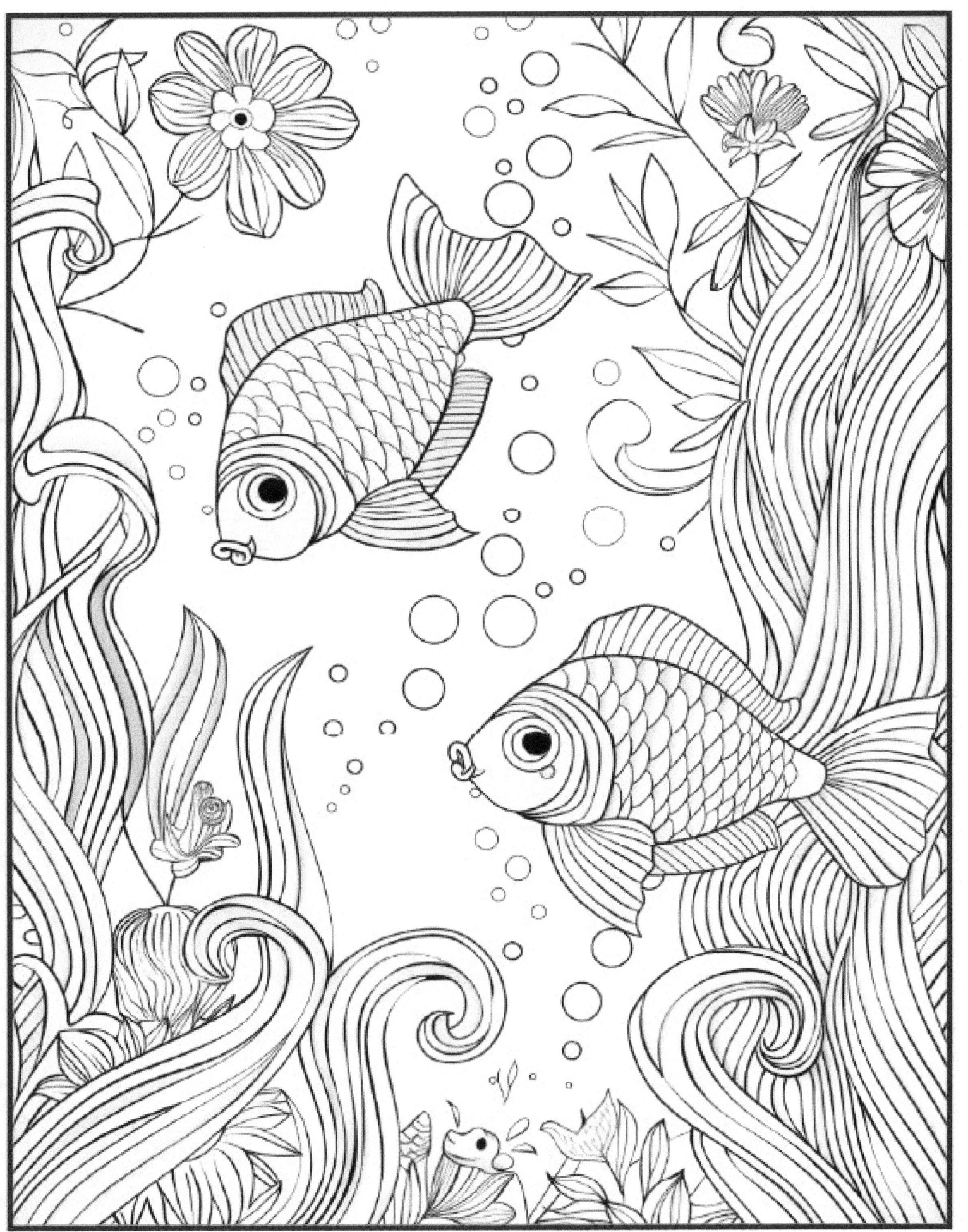

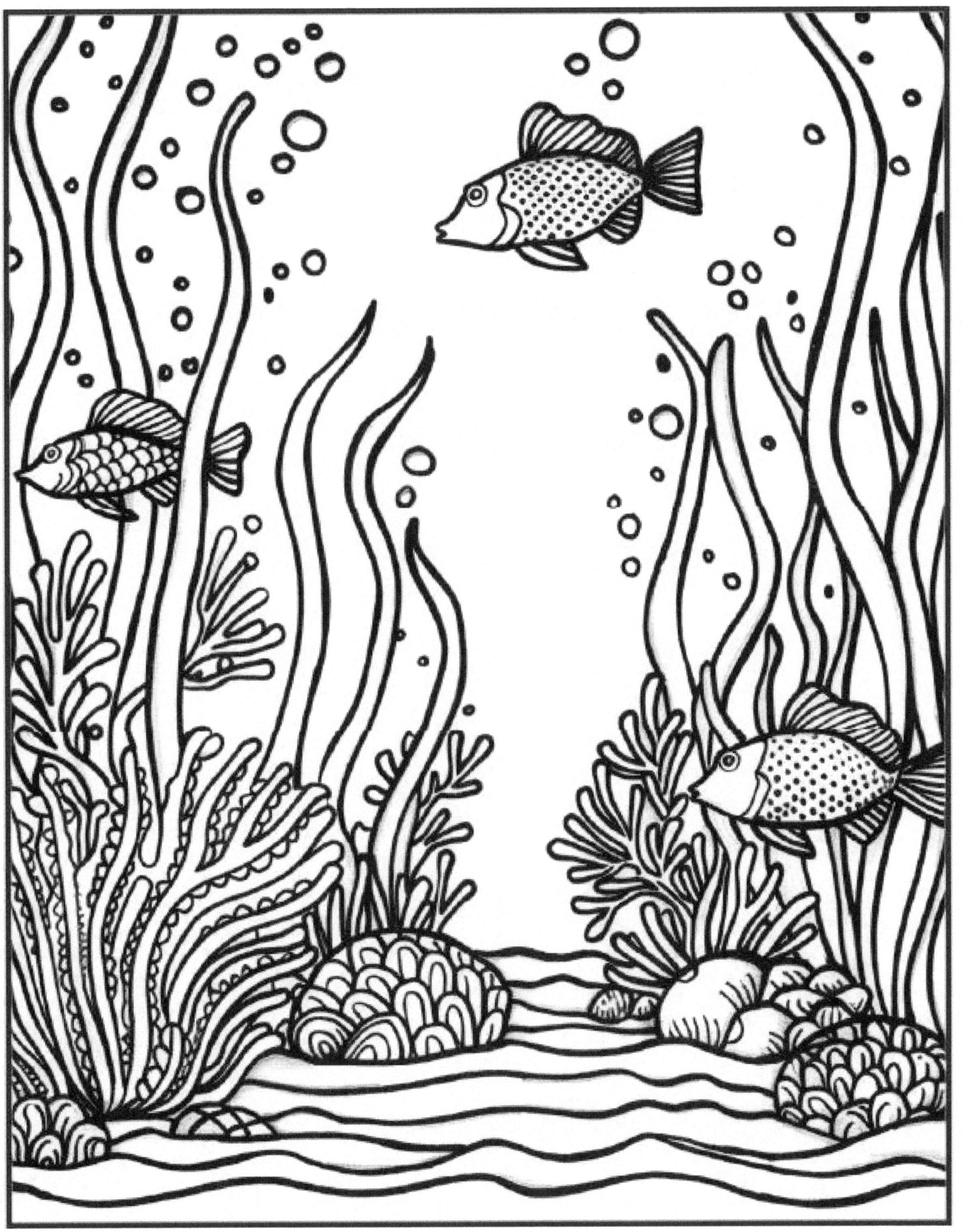

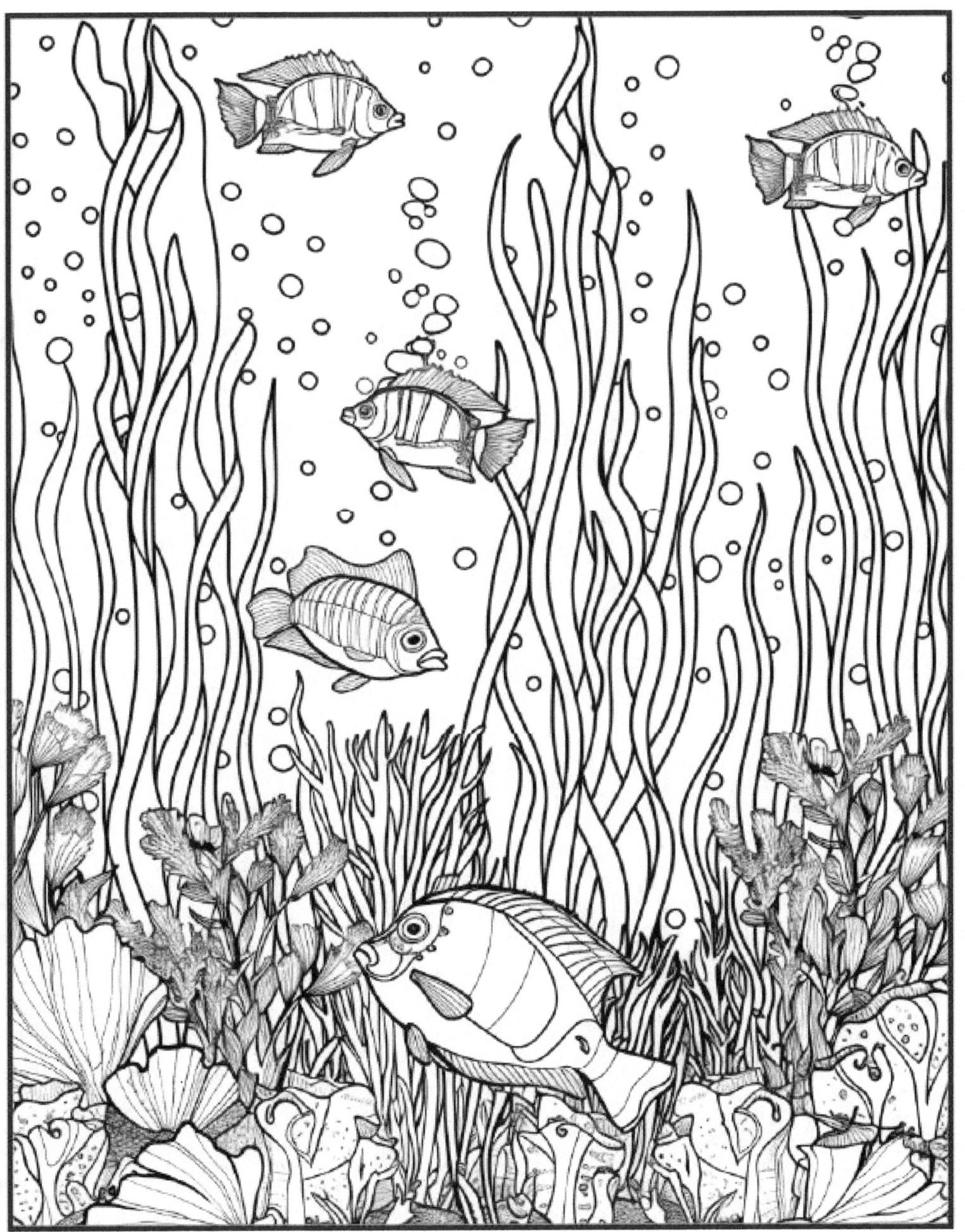

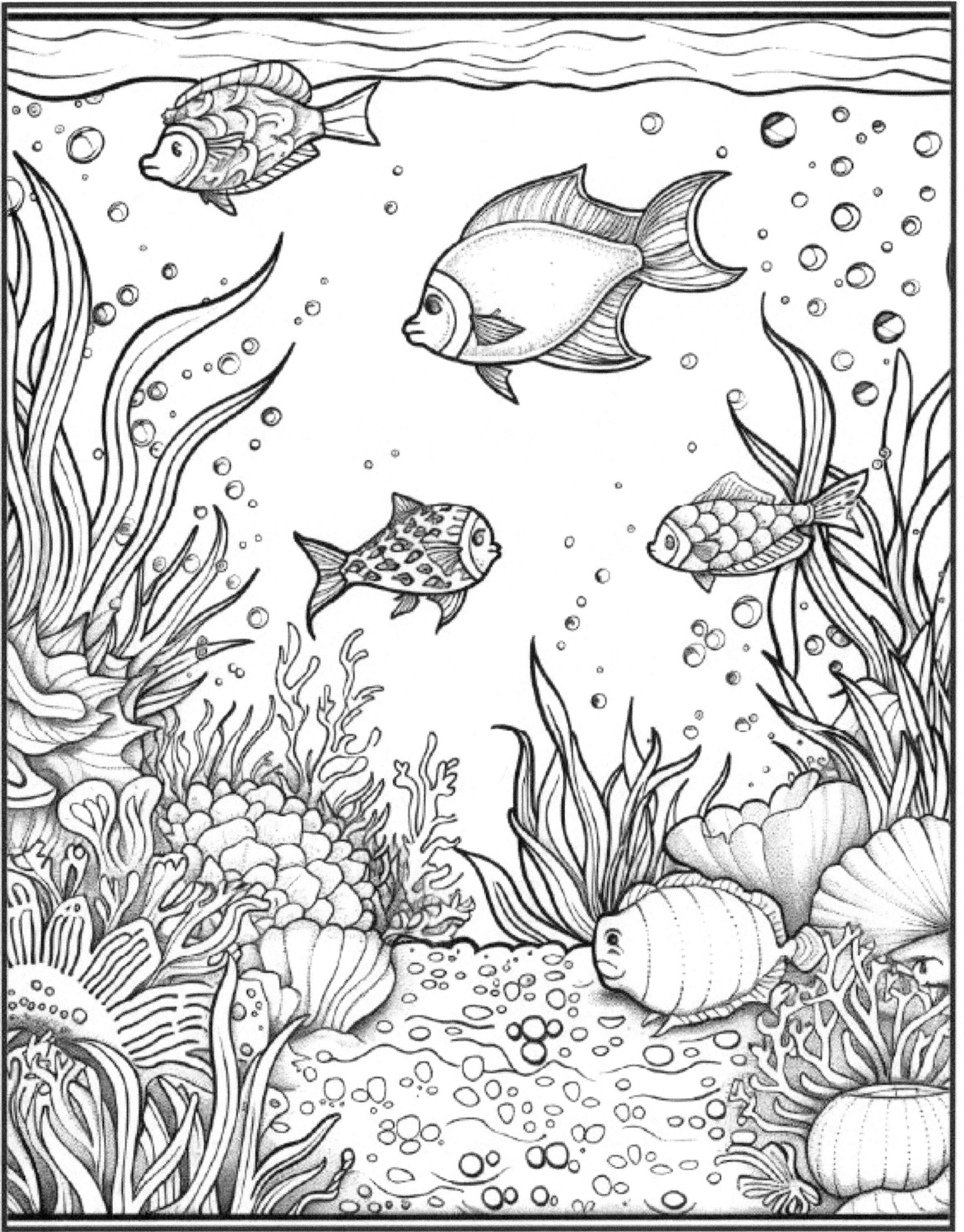

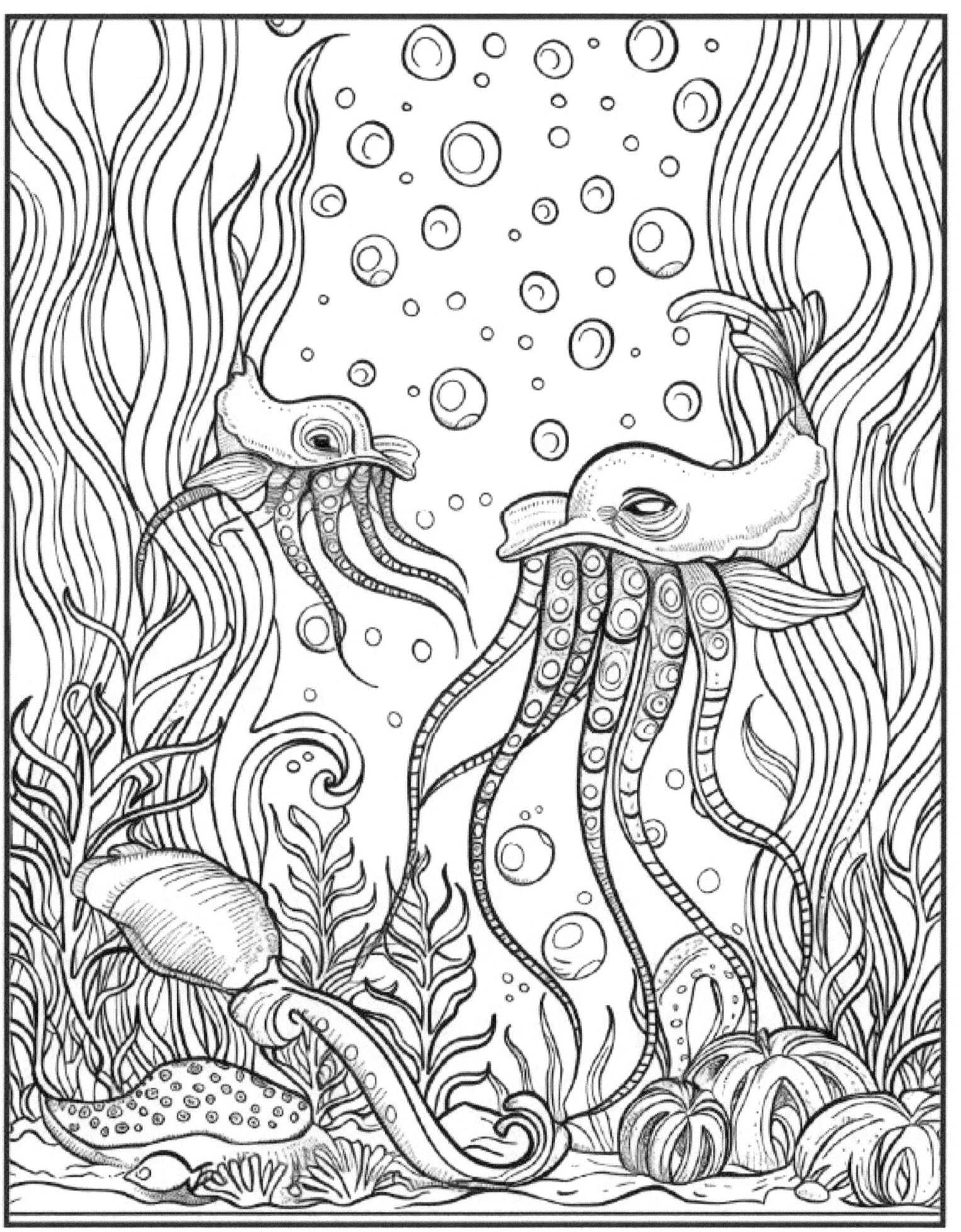

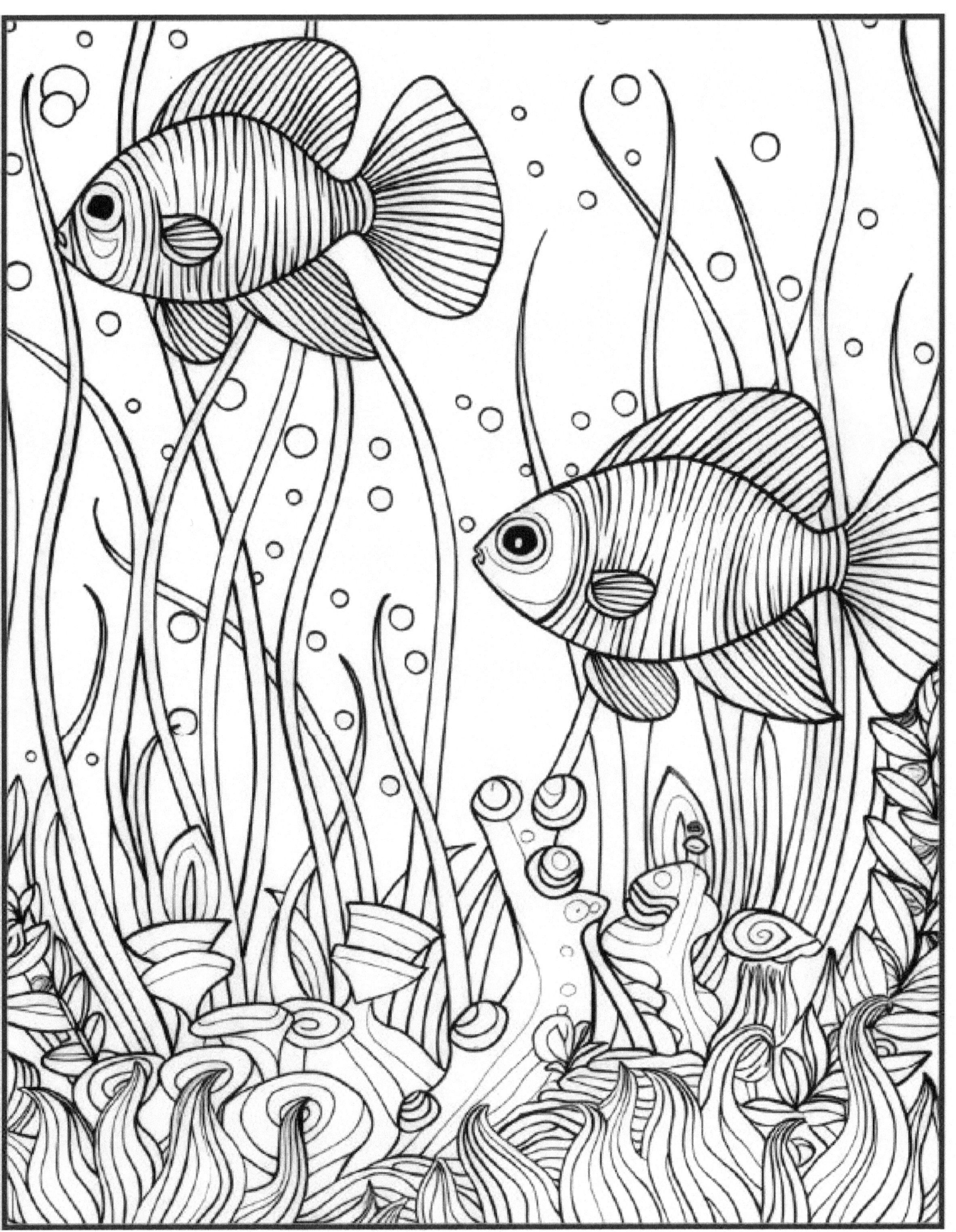

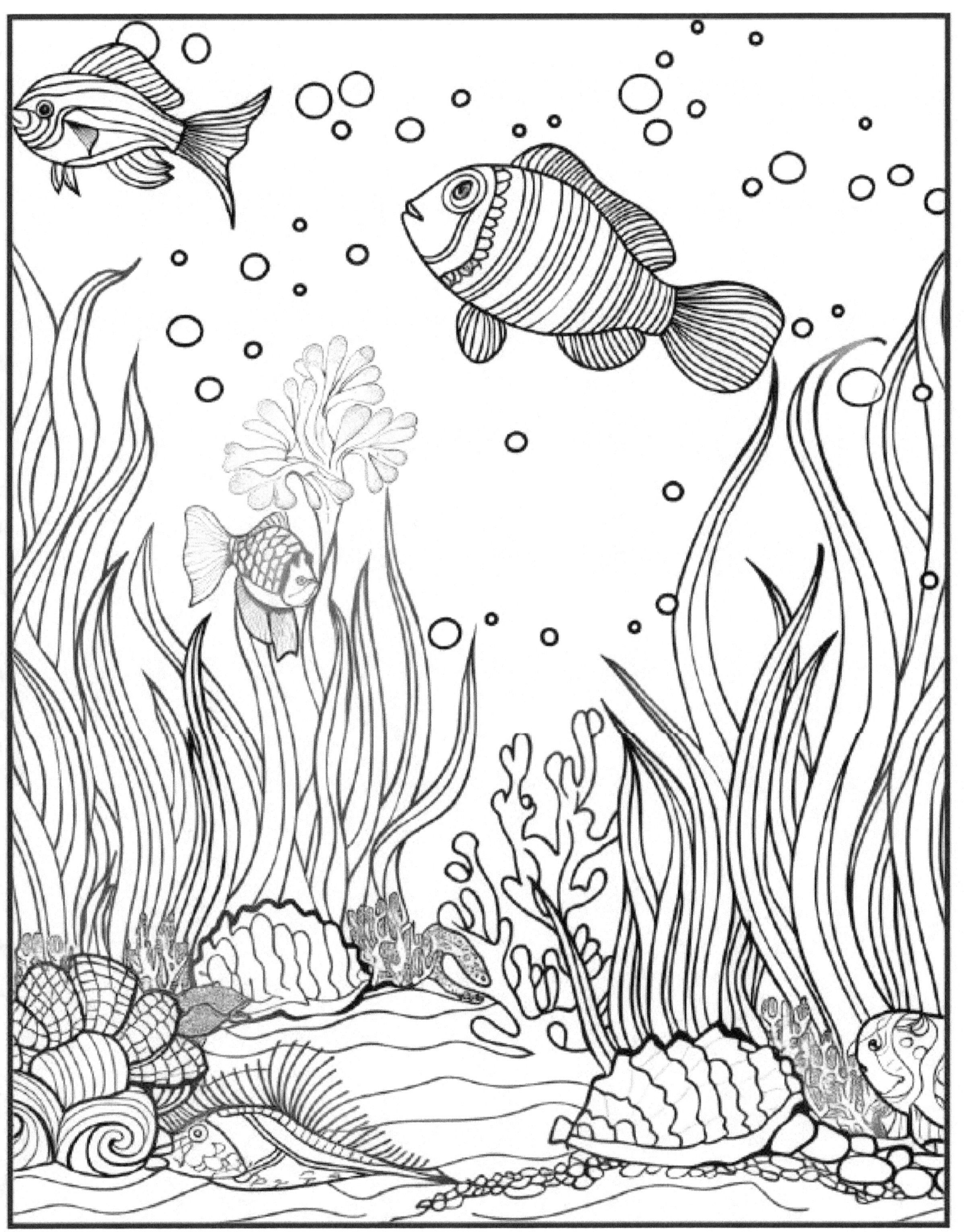

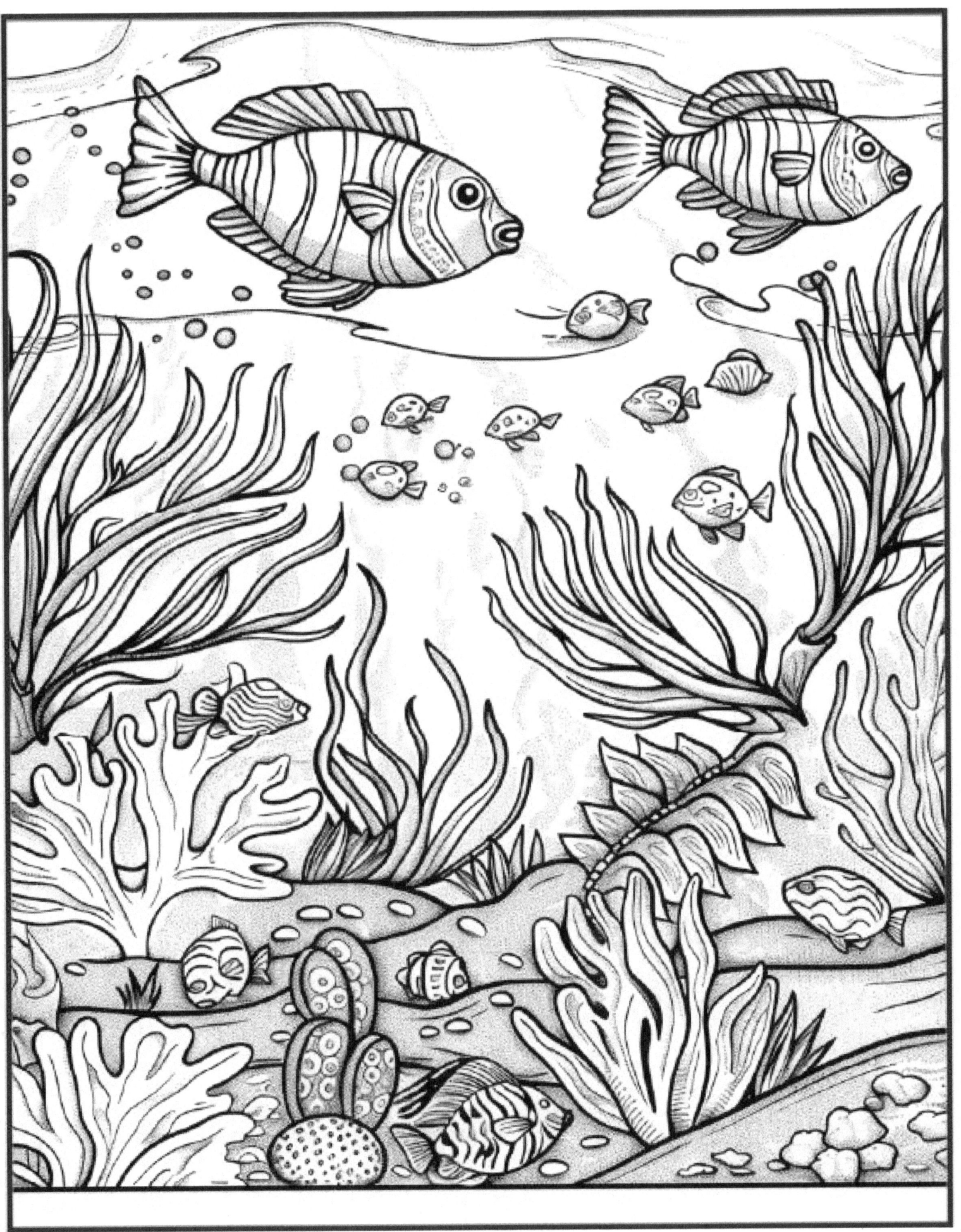

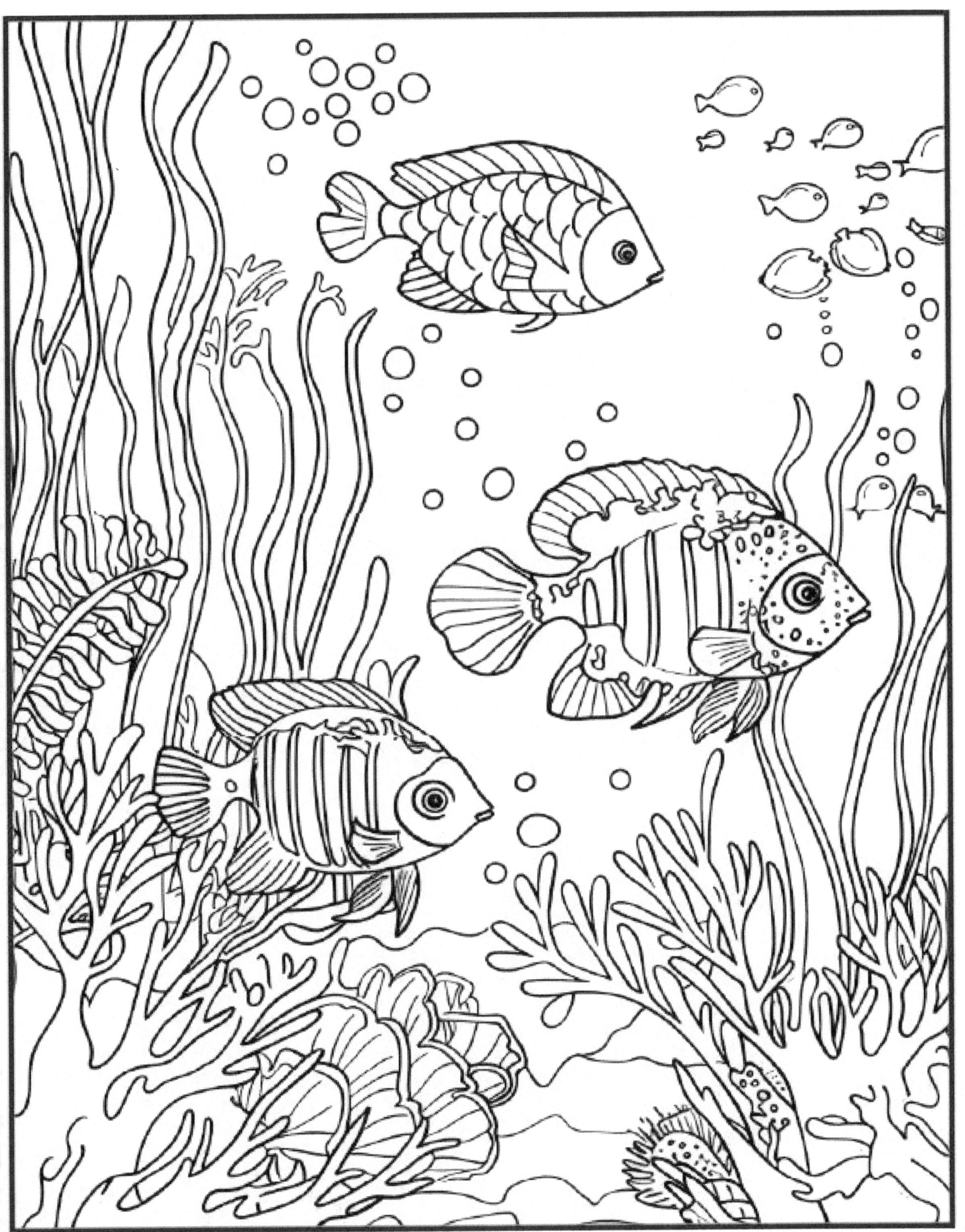

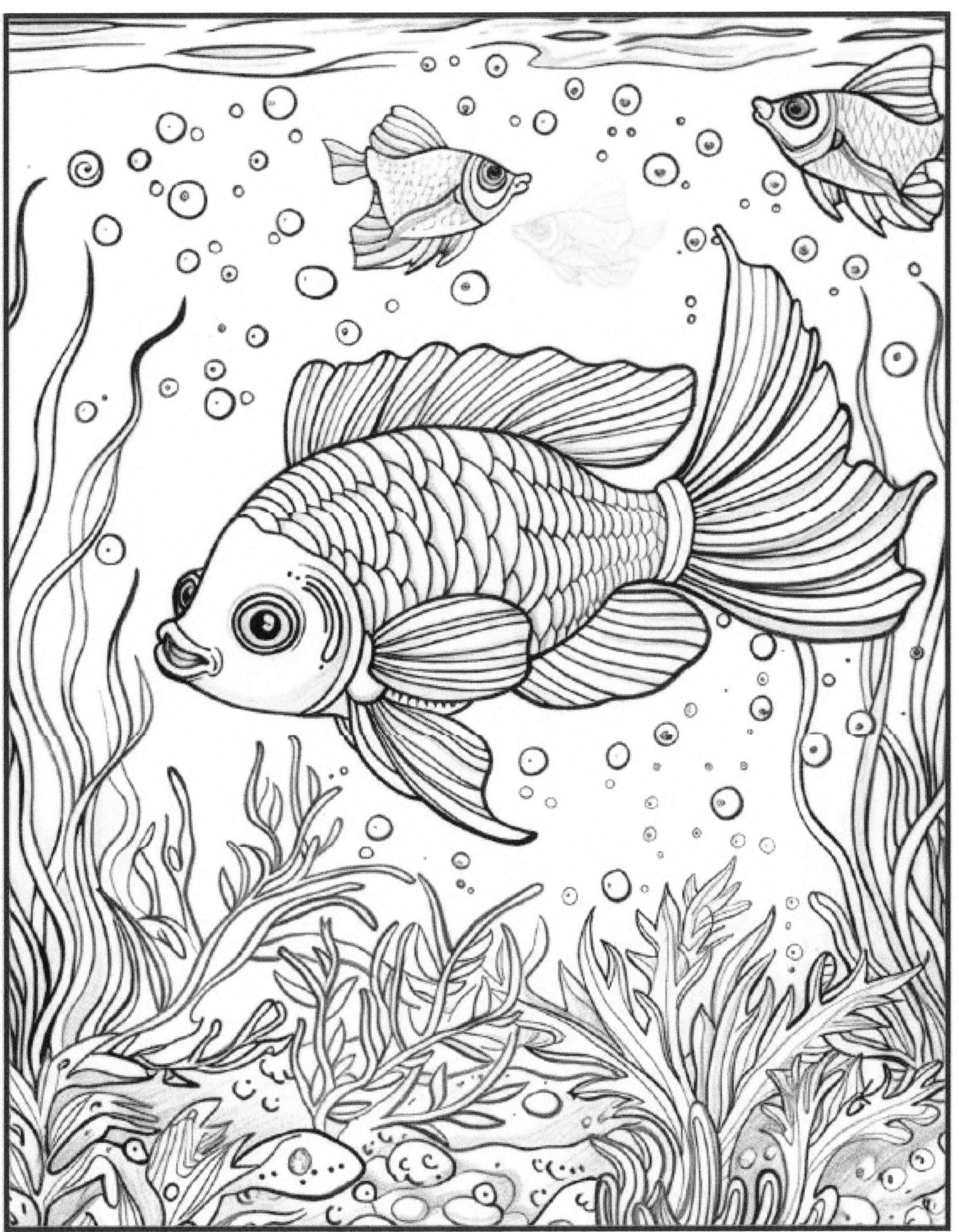

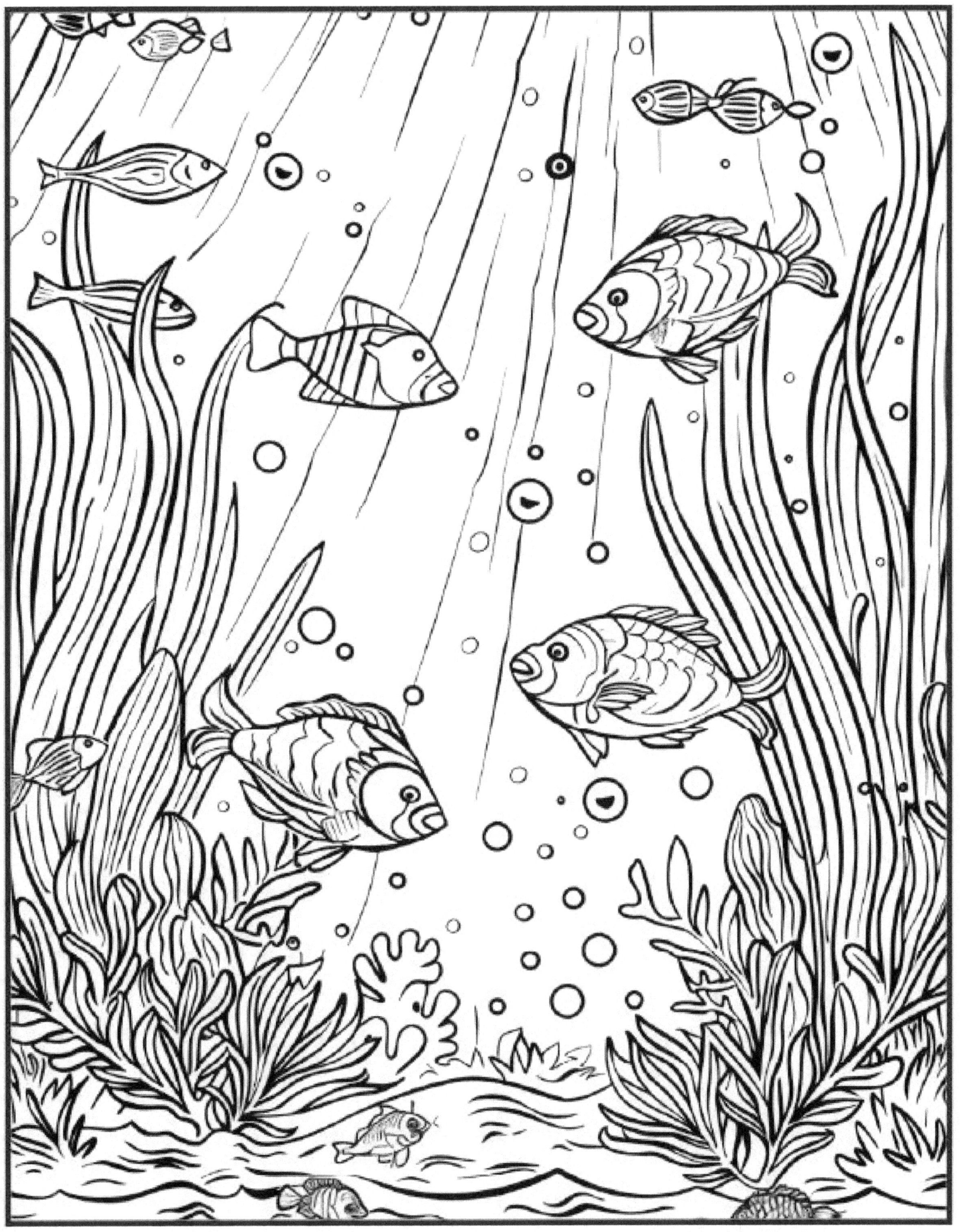

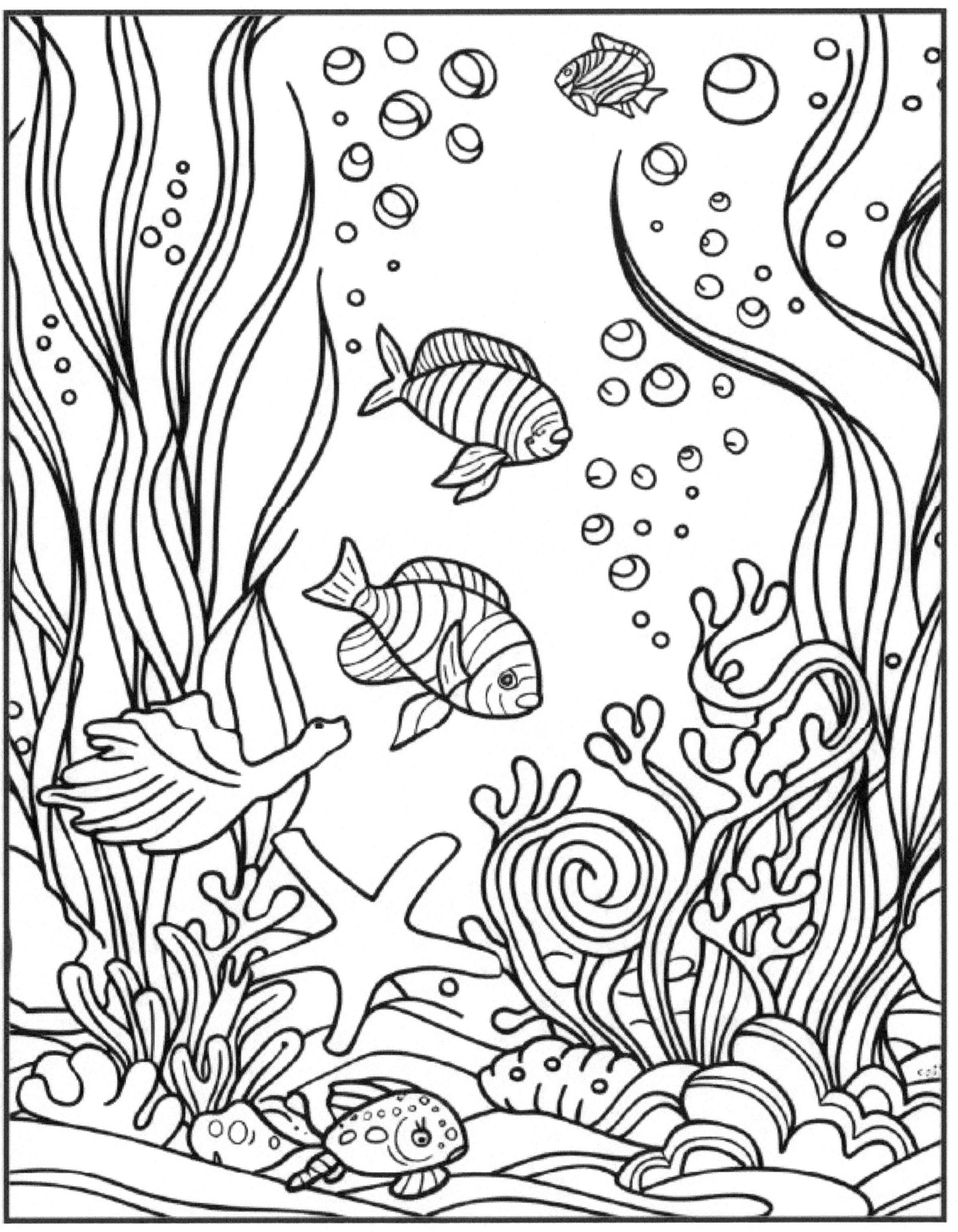

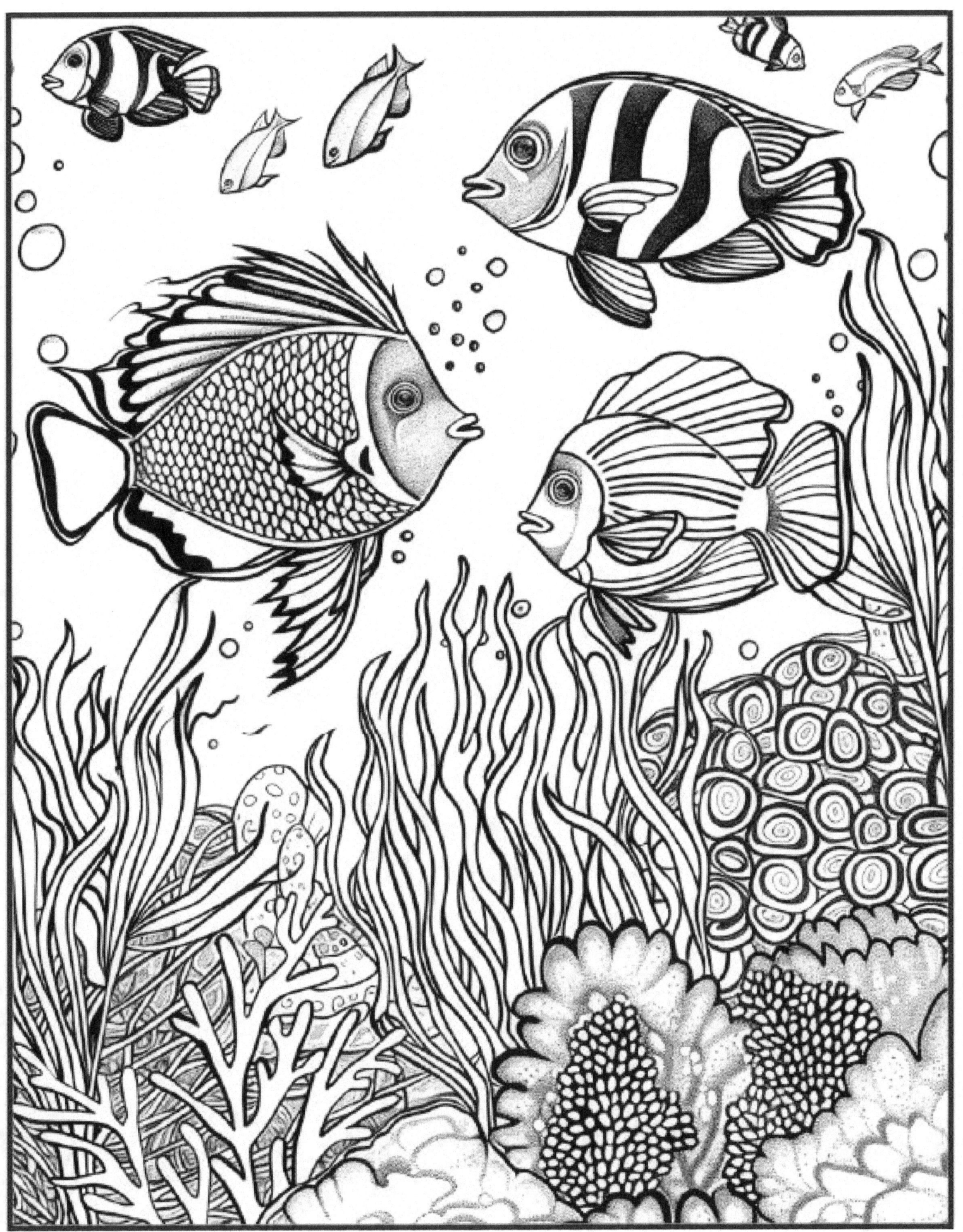

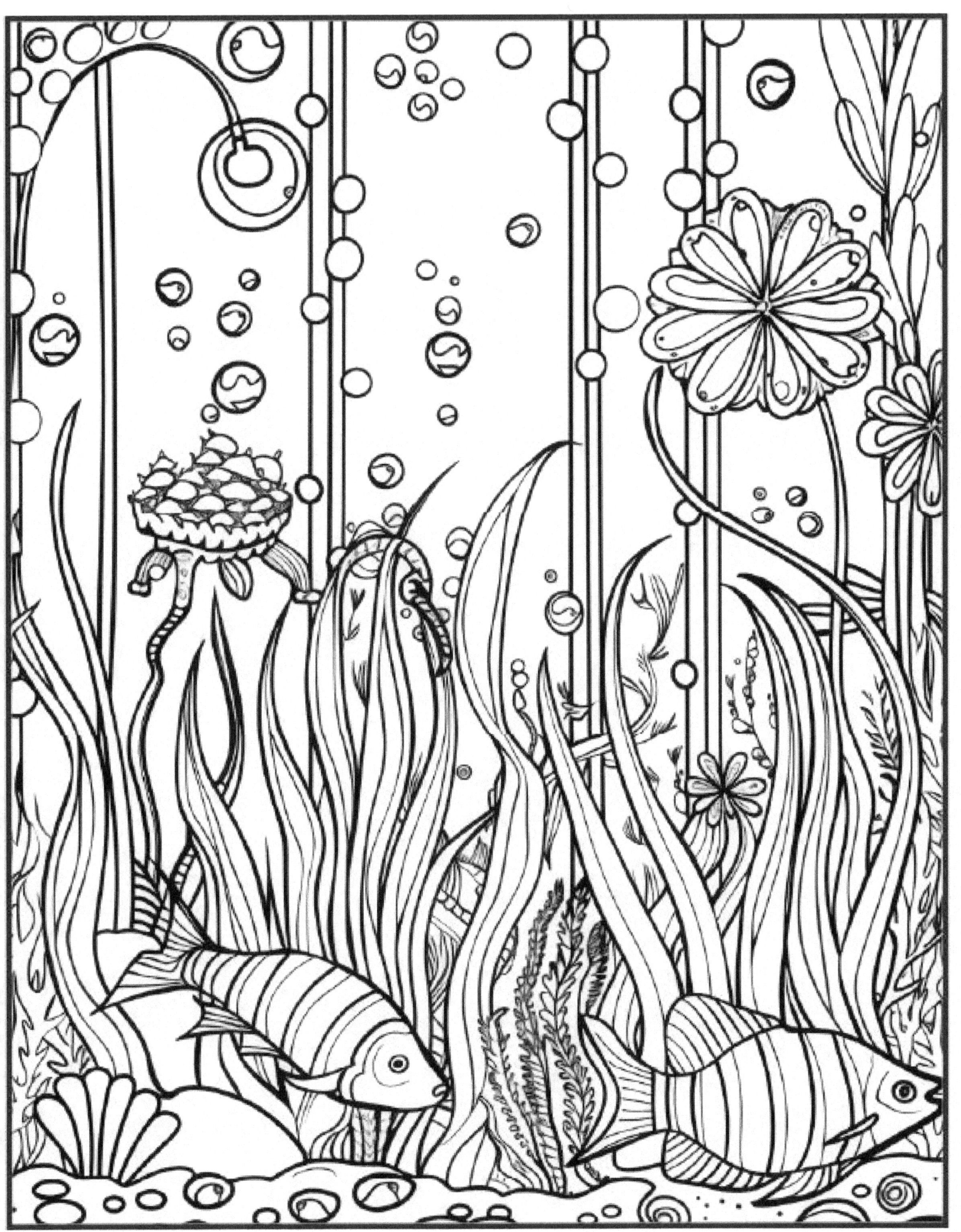

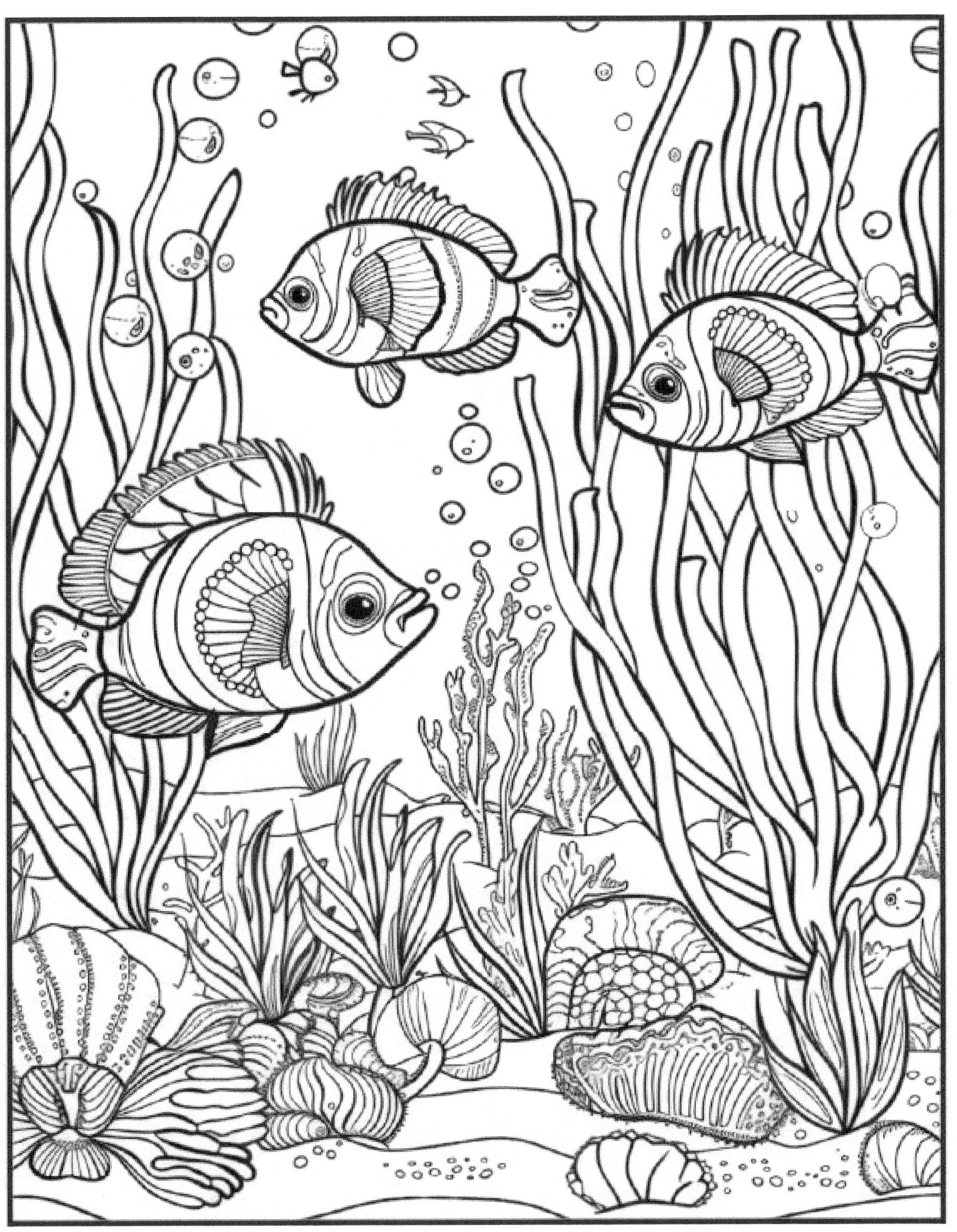

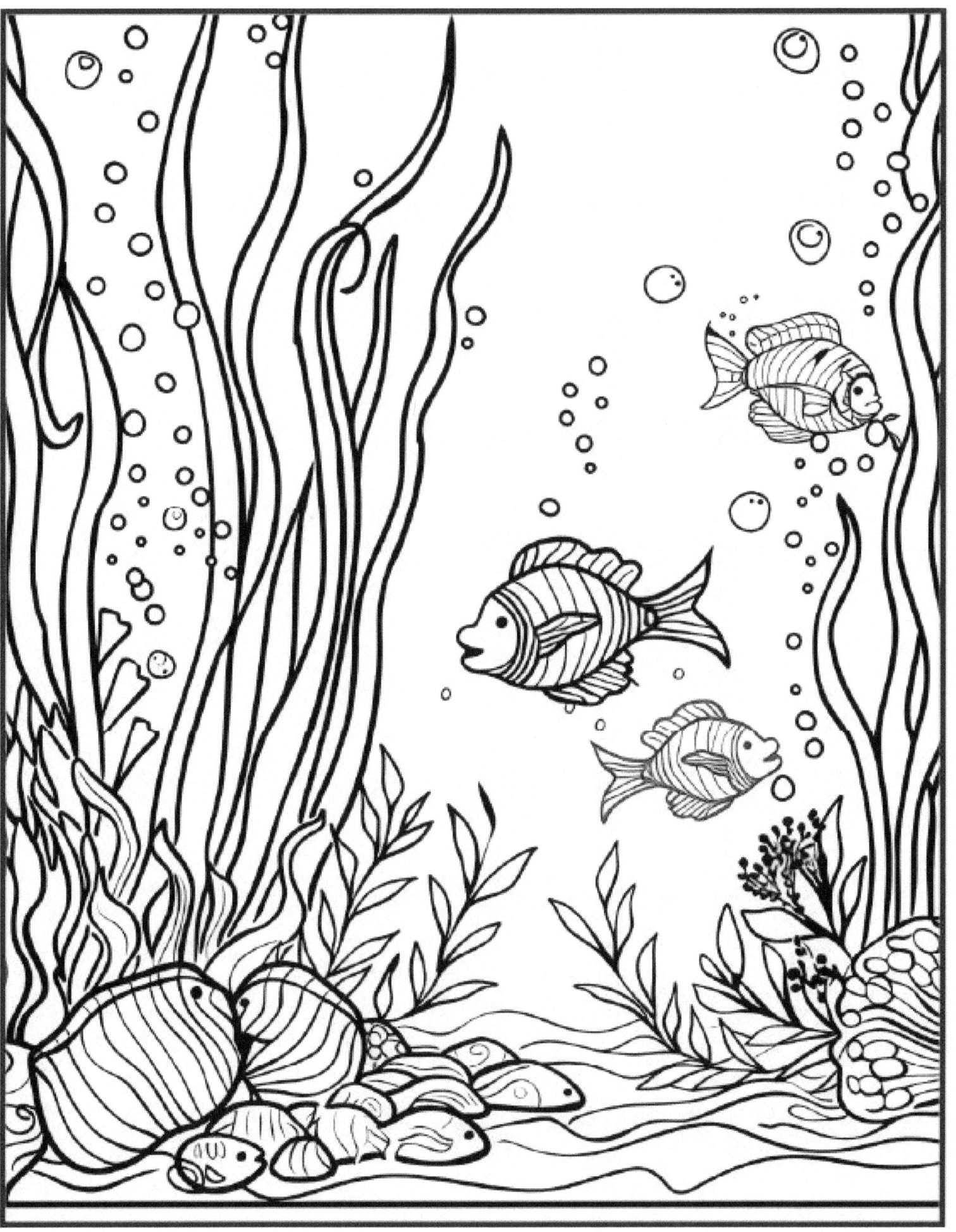

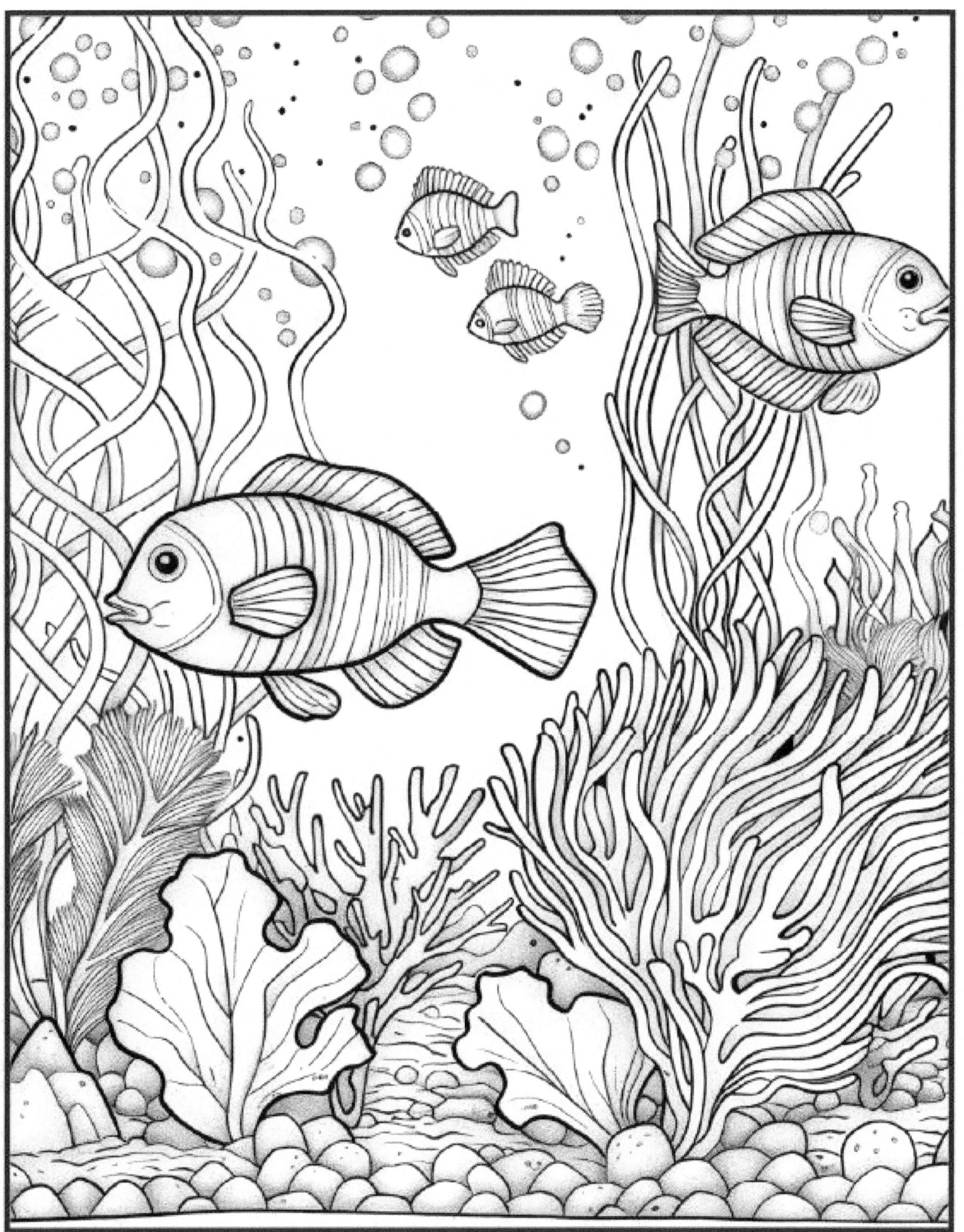

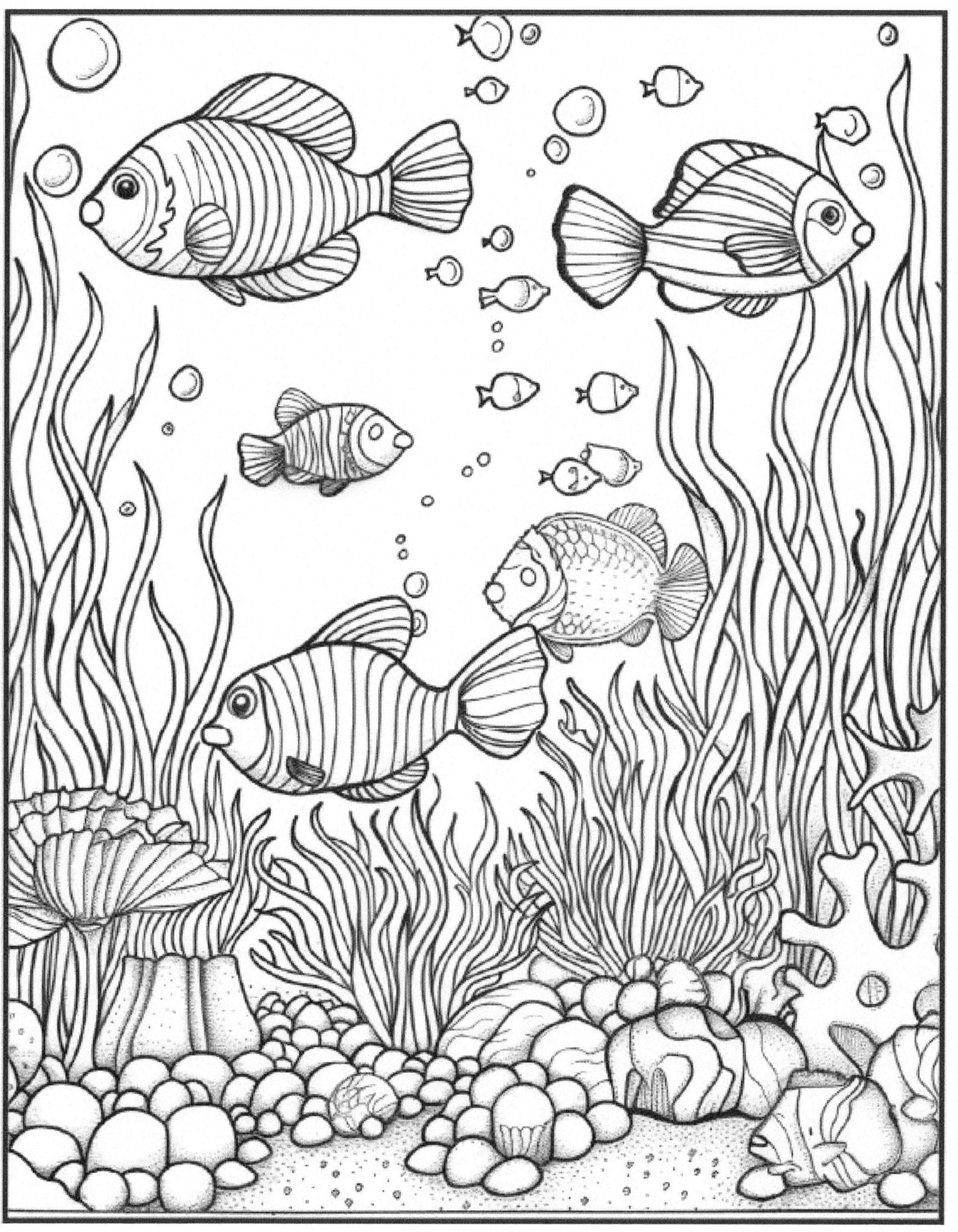

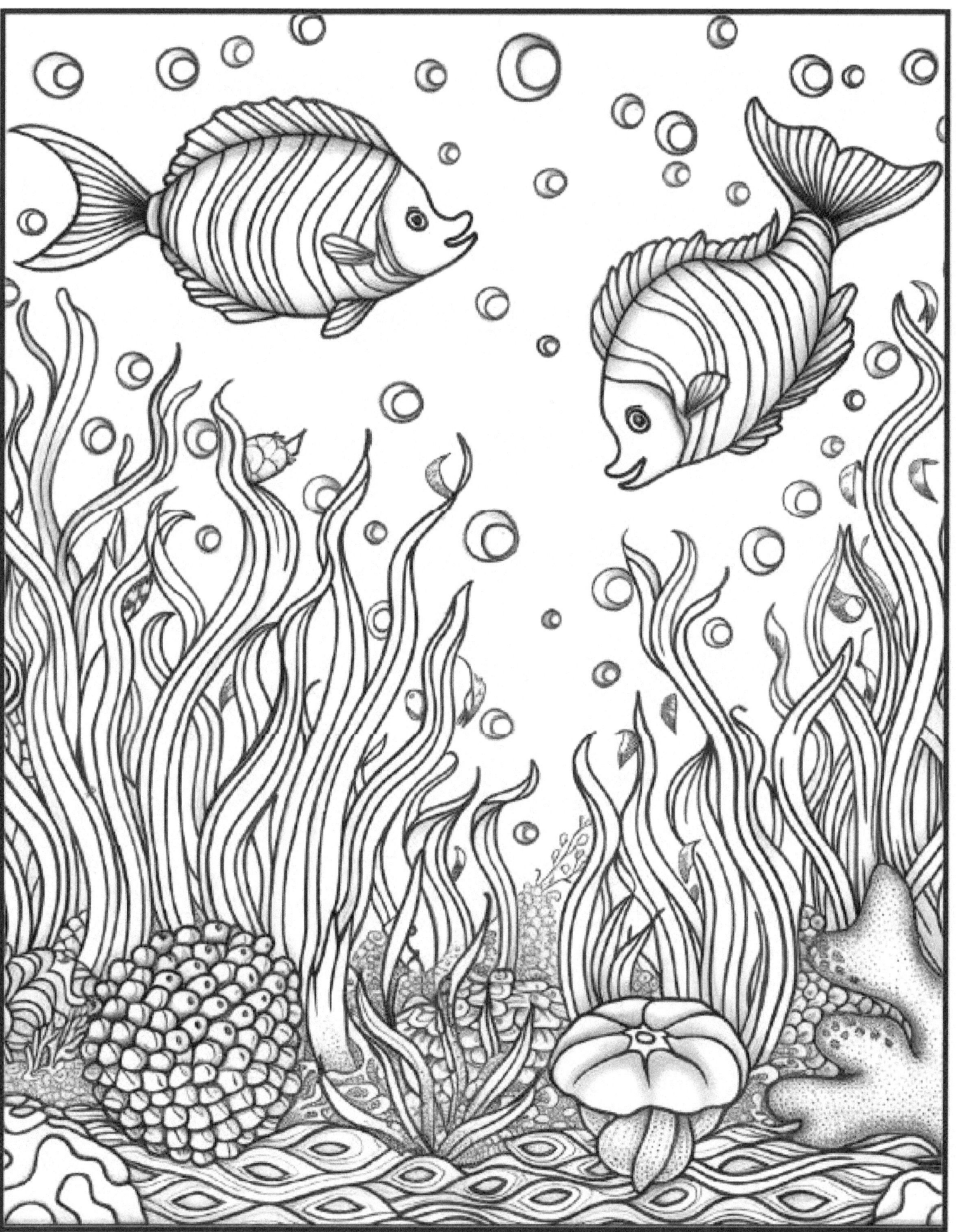

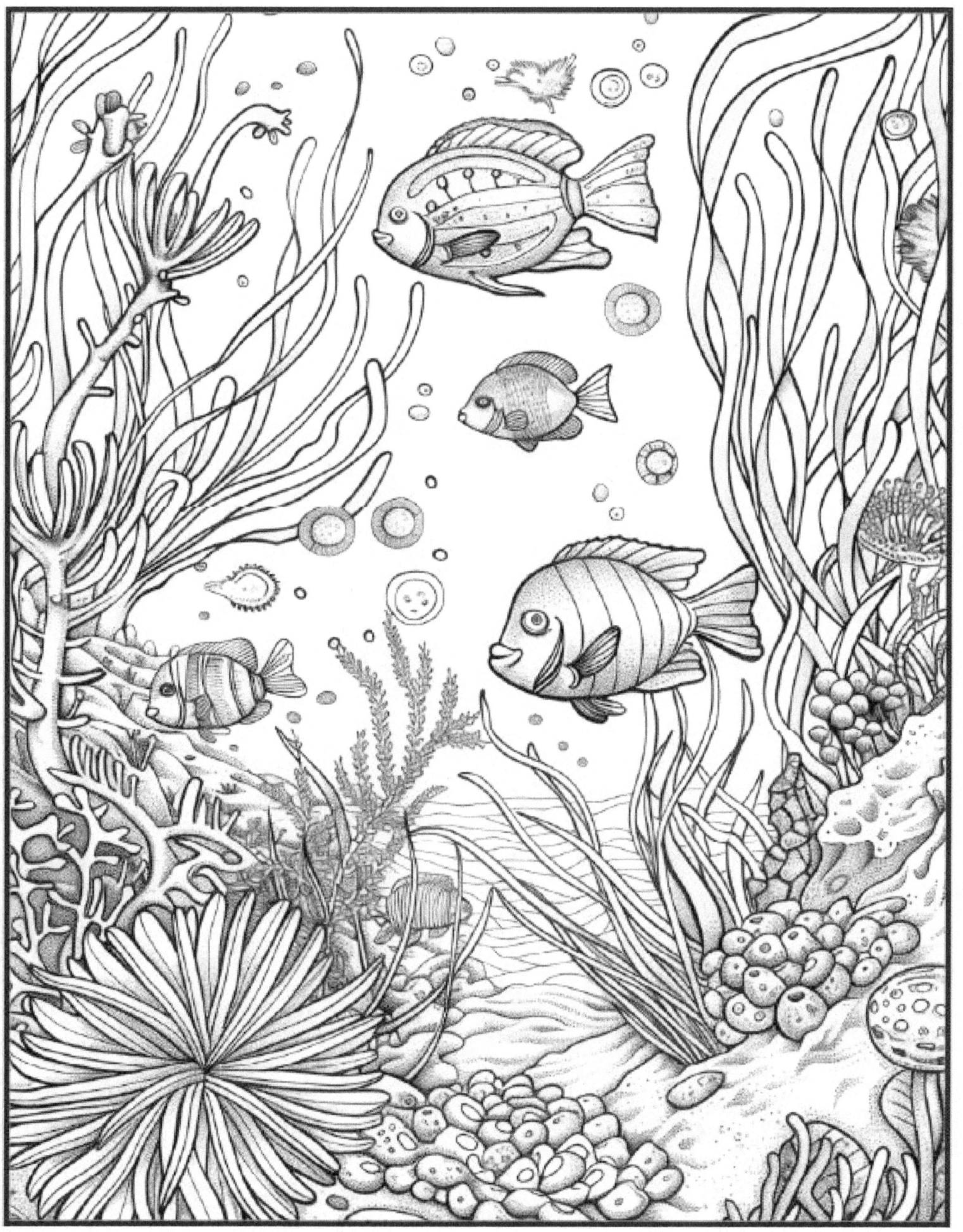

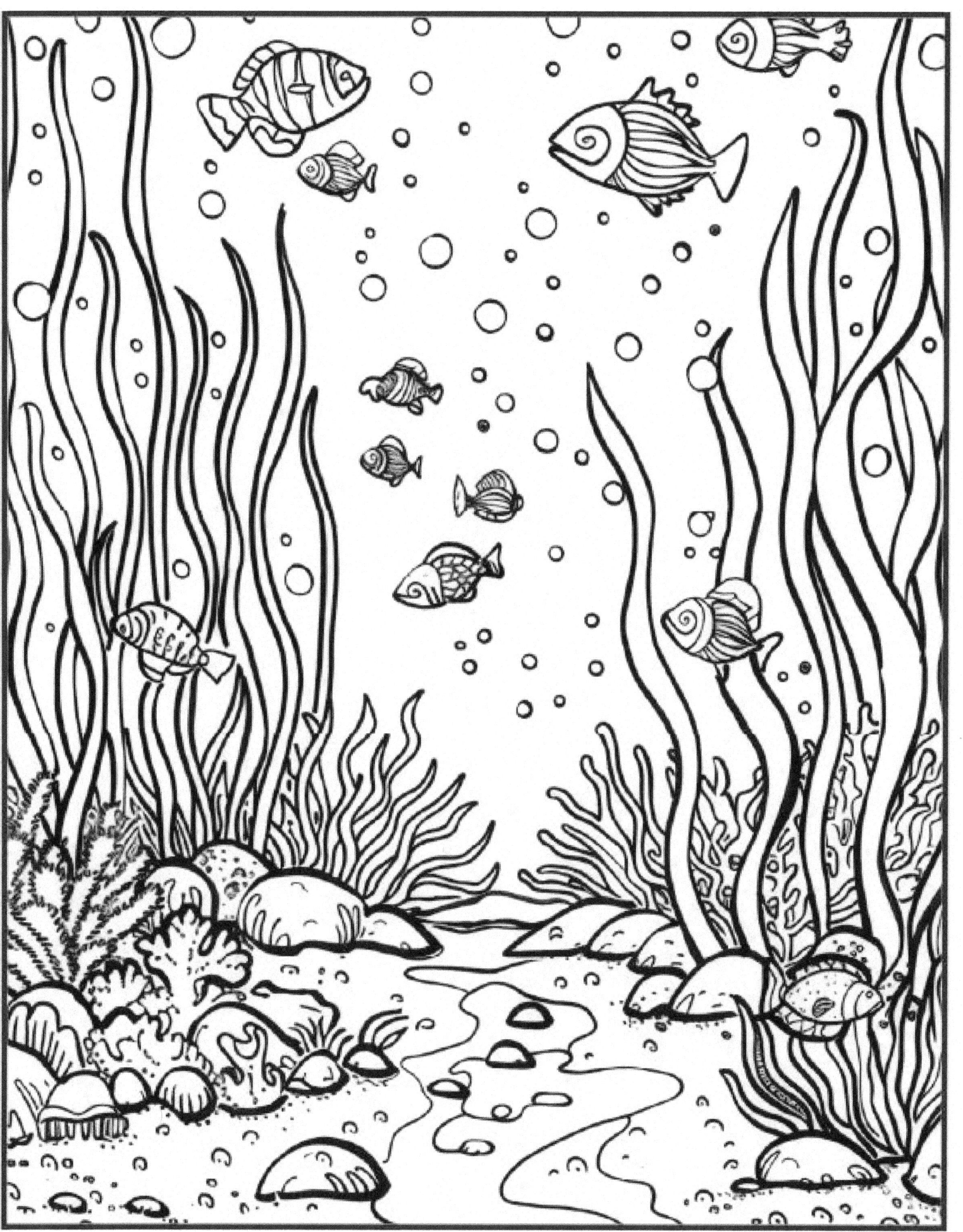

# ColorQuest Collections

**Fun and creative coloring books**

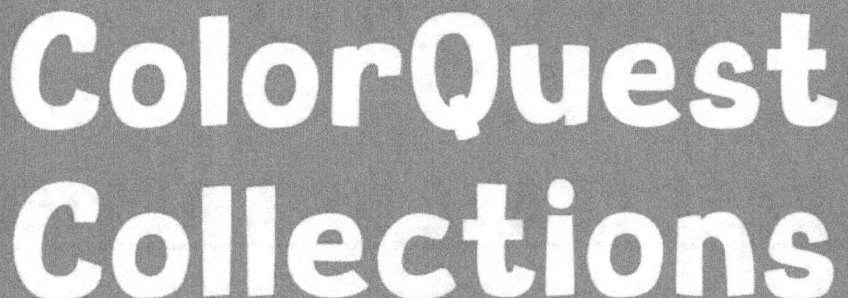

**Calming | Relaxing | Stress Relief**

For more fun and creative coloring books, search for ColorQuest Collections in your favorite bookstore!

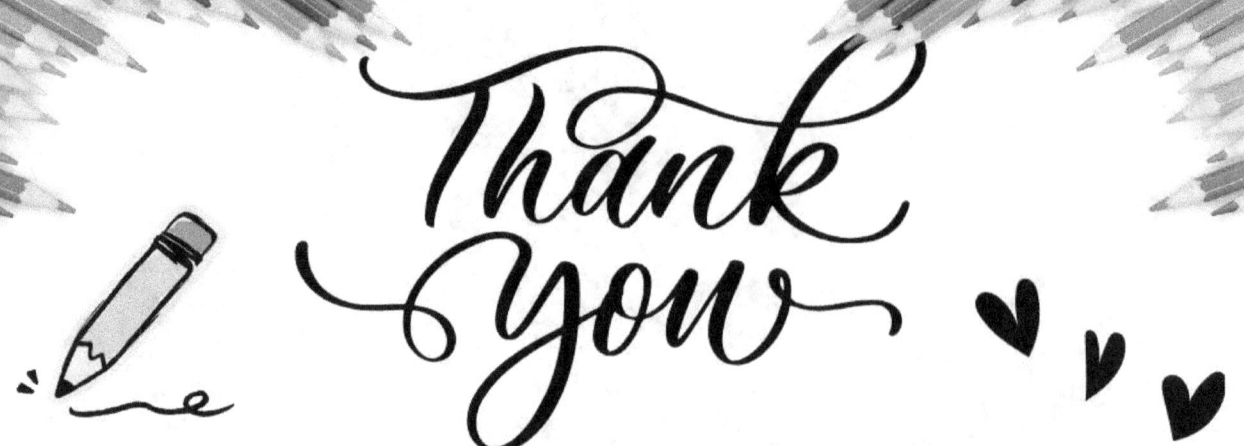

# Thank You

# PLEASE LEAVE US A REVIEW!

IF YOU ENJOYED THIS COLORING BOOK, PLEASE TAKE A MOMENT TO LEAVE A REVIEW. YOUR FEEDBACK HELPS US IMPROVE AND GUIDES OTHER CREATIVE SPIRITS TO THEIR PERFECT COLORING ADVENTURE!

## SCAN HERE

FOR MORE CREATIVE COLORING BOOKS, PLEASE SEARCH FOR COLORQUEST COLLECTIONS IN YOUR FAVORITE BOOKSTORE!

# COLORQUEST COLLECTIONS

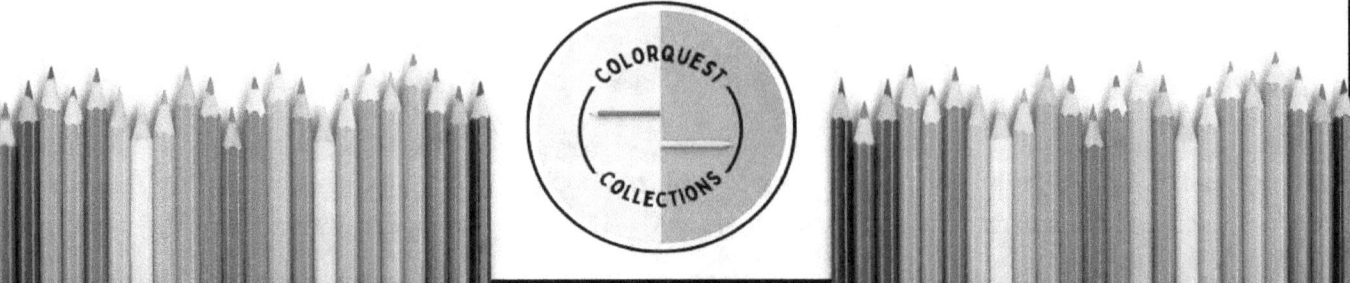